All Weather Whitetails

Forecasting Your Next Hunt of a Lifetime

by

Jeff Sturgis

Edited by
Mavis Sturgis

11-10-18
Now find whitetail
Success
by
weather!

Whitetail Habitat Solutions, LLC
206 School Street
Coon Valley, WI 54623
www.whitetailhabitatsolutions.com

Ordering Information:
Quantity sales. Special discounts are available on quantity purchases by corporations, associations, and others. For details, contact the publisher at the address above.

Orders by U.S. trade bookstores and wholesalers.
Whitetail Habitat Solutions, LLC:
Tel: (608) 452-2632; or visit:
www.whitetailhabitatsolutions.com

All photos used in this publication were provided by the author, or used by permission from the following individuals, including: Dylan Lenz from Black Stamp Media and Cory Wiedel

Printed in the United States of America

ISBN 978-0-9882900-4-4

Dedication

Throughout the decades there have been so many hunting buddies that I have shared memories to last a lifetime with. My father, my sons including Jake, Dante and Sam, and even my brother Kevin, who was one of my first hunting buddies when we weren't even old enough to drive, back in the mid-80s. I was honored to share hunting trips with Skip Rutter, Ross Fernandez, Colin Svum, Dave Larson, Aaron Pilger, Jim Morrow, Mark Thomas, Devon Sturgis, Dave Potts, Max Palmreuter, Paul Keller Tex Laidler, John Lapine, John Pratt and Bill Hawkins. I can't stand naming names because I am certain I will miss a few. Dylan Lenz and now Mike Mancl who have been a couple of highly skilled camera men that I have shared a few trees with and who I also now consider my friends. I was even honored to enjoy a few hunts with the late Bob Potts, who was one of my earliest hunting mentors and a man I deeply respected. However, there were a few select hunting buddies who have had to put up with me the most, and who have allowed me the privilege of hunting with them, for many years.

Although it has been too many years, Mike Pratt began taking me hunting with him before I could even take drivers training, let alone drive myself. Karl Keller has hunted with me off and on since the mid 90s and I'm not sure I know anyone who has actually shot more whitetails than he has. Joe Lasak hunted with me for 7 years in PA during his first out-of-state deer hunts, and now I'm pretty certain he has killed more deer in more states than I have. Rich Ghekiere has turned into a close friend and has put up with me the most lately, hunting 4 years in WI, then 4 years in OH and then back again for a year in WI in 2018. Last but not least there is Tim Glover who has been a buddy since the early 2000s. I was only honored enough to spend a few years hunting with, however, Tim's trusted friendship has traveled well beyond the hunts.

During all of our hunting adventures, it was the shared passion for hunting whitetails that built friendship, respect and a common brotherhood that non-hunters could never understand. At times I know I was too strict with scent control, being quiet, rotating stands, hanging stands, sitting on time and of course, hunting purely by the weather forecast. I know I struggled with at least 1 hunting buddy because I preferred to drive 7 hours one way to hunt for 1 day of great weather during the middle of the week, rather than hunting a long weekend during poor weather conditions. At times, I have followed the "hunting rules", along with the weather forecast, so strictly that I forgot about being the best hunting buddy that I could be. It is a good thing this is a forgiving bunch!

My best friend and latest hunting buddy has had to put up with me the most – my wife, Diane. As I write this, she is sitting during a 22 degree start to the day, in a treestand that took her ½ hour to hike into, up-hill. I can honestly say that hunting whitetails lately has been a blessing to our relationship.

Friendship, memories to last a lifetime and even a level of forgiveness towards this crabby, middle-aged nimrod who has used the weather and other hunting rules on the side of obsessiveness at times...are the reasons why I dedicate this book to all of YOU! For what kind of hunters would we be, without our treasured hunting buddies....

Table of Contents

Acknowledgments

Why do whitetails do this, and why ***do*** whitetails ***do that***? All whitetail hunters have gone through the list of hundreds of questions like an excited 7-year old: Why, why, why? Endlessly! However, unlike a 7-year old who typically has a father, a mentor or a teacher around to definitively answer why about anything and everything – many whitetail hunters have never had that trusted source to answer their burning questions when it comes to anything whitetail. Nearly 20 years ago I was fortunate to find my whitetail "why" person, and even more fortunate to spend nearly a decade asking any whitetail question that I could think of. In fact, this individual I acknowledged in a previous book, and in my experience, I am not sure that there has been a greater authority on scientifically proven whitetail behavior. Ever!

After a long career as a Whitetail Research Biologist with the State of Michigan, and with dozens of peer-reviewed articles to his credit, John Ozoga was the why person for hundreds of thousands of folks for many years as the Research Editor for Deer and Deer Hunting magazine. In fact, I have heard that John is the most quoted, peer reviewed research biologist ever. John was the person who would take an article that had been contributed about whitetails for publication in Deer and Deer hunting magazine, he would then cross out words, phrases and paragraphs in red, add notes, make corrections, and then send it back to be changed and published. I feel in a verbally kind, authoritative, and in a personal way, John Ozoga crossed out some of my ideas, added notes and made corrections.

During one of my first conversations with John, he set me straight about the moon and its lack of any influence on the timing of the rut, based on decades of ultrasound, date-of-conception research. Then came the weather. John revealed to me that although there could be an increase or decrease in daylight rutting activity based on the weather, the weather, was not responsible for the timing of the rut. However, I took the potential association of increased daylight deer movements, based on some kind of set of weather factors, and ran with it. That conversation helped to confirm everything that I had already been observing for more than a decade. That conversation was during the late 90s, and although I can't quote John, and my memory is foggy that far back, John really kicked my obsession with deer and the weather forecast into overdrive. I was extremely excited and whether John knows it or not, he created a deer forecasting junkie of enormous magnitude.

John, I have thanked you before and I need to thank you again! Referring to you as my whitetail "why person" doesn't even come close to reflecting the numerous lifetime achievement awards and what you have contributed to the entire world of whitetails, including whitetail herds, hunters, and to those who have entrenched their careers within all things whitetail, like myself.

It is with a considerate level of respect that I acknowledge and send you my deepest and heartfelt ***Thank You***, to you, John Ozoga.

Foreword

In the spring of 2013, I reached out to some guy who ran a Whitetail blogging website and property consultation business, in hopes of finding insight on how to make a living in the Whitetail world. At the time, I had no idea who Jeff Sturgis really was or what Whitetail Habitat Solutions was, for that matter, but I figured that anyone with that many bucks on the wall and stories to tell had to be the real deal. Several years later I was still job hopping, trying to decide how I could make my passion a career, when out of the blue I got a call from Jeff. Less than a month later, everything I owned was packed up to move across the state to work side by side with the man himself.

Admittedly, I was a greenhorn when it came to mature buck hunting, and I'm sure Jeff knew that from the bat. Over the months, now years, he described and elaborated in excruciating detail more Whitetail knowledge than my mind could ever soak up. However, the elements that have fascinated me most and stuck in my mind, involve weather and deer movement. To me, it was always an oversight. Go sit, put your time in, and you are bound to get lucky at some point or another. But Jeff helped me realize that there is much more to it than that. Conditions are an enormous influence on potential success in the woods, and Jeff seems to understand the ins and outs of those influences. His track record certainly suggests so.

With a proven record of high level success that leaves no shred of doubt, Jeff has learned through trial and error, the ins and outs of mature buck hunting. He'll be the first to tell you that analyzing the weather and hunting accordingly, has everything to do with finding consistent success in the deer woods. It's an eye-opening realization that is incredibly underestimated. His insight and advice on utilizing the weather to harvest mature bucks will forever change the way you hunt.

As I currently sit, just 3 feet over his shoulder in The Upper Point Stand - one of our favorite sets to hunt while waiting for cruising bucks to pass by, our hopes are high. The conditions are optimal, and we've already seen a handful of deer on the move; it's just a matter of time before a mature buck slips into sight. Jeff is all the reason we are here. The weather helped him choose the day, the time and the location. I am glad he chose me to come along for the ride.

Introduction

The date was November 20th, 2016, the 2nd day of Wisconsin's gun season, and over a 2-day period the weather had taken one of the most drastic turns in recent deer season memory. A 40-degree temperature drop and wind speeds that decreased over 30mph in just 48 hours, created the conditions for memories to last a lifetime in the deer blind.

"There he is again – shoot!", I whispered to my stepson Dante. I fumbled to turn on the camera and managed to turn the on/off button to view, instead of record; amateur! The camera didn't matter though, because making sure that Dante got a shot at his first buck was the priority of this fleeting moment. The buck stood above us on the oak filled finger ridge, just 30 yards away. Dante moved slowly into position in the pop-up blind and fired! The buck kicked and ran less than 100 yards to his death. As I followed Dante through the low-wooded hardwood valley and towards a bench below a rocky point, the movement was very welcome during the frosty morning temperatures. Neither of us knew for sure the buck had expired. As Dante slowly climbed to the top of the bench and moved across the flat below the rocks where my son Jake had shot a beautiful 9-point during a snow-filled opener in 2015, the fist pump and grin from ear to ear, delivered the incredible conclusion to the story of another cold front buck for the memory books. However, the rewards from the extreme weather that eventually delivered this buck to the dinner table, were only getting started.

Since the mid 80s I have experienced, enjoyed and lived an accumulation of hunting weather factors that have defined not only how I currently hunt, but how I manage a professional whitetail career, family, friends and a whitetail life that often extends to a full 7 days per week. I have written this book because the roller coaster of weather extremities has been at the center of it all. The whitetail deerfront hunting strategies that I discuss in the following chapters aren't just tips that I have tried for a few years, or a decade or two. Instead, these are tactics that I have recognized, relied upon, refined and reaffirmed, since I first learned to drive a car in 1986. Years ago I began writing about, and later creating videos, to explain how hunters can use the weather to predict exactly when they should climb into their favorite treestand. In the November 2015 rut issue of October Life, I released my whitetail rut formula so that hunters can calculate their own high value dates to hunt, often a week or more into the future. To say that these weather-related concepts can change your success as a hunter, while helping you balance the true priorities in life all at the same time, is a drastic understatement. This book is long overdue.

The same passion that I approach teaching how to read and forecast your next great high value whitetail opportunity based on the weather, is the same level of passion that I continued to attack that outstanding deerfront which first delivered Dante's buck during the middle of November, 2016. After field dressing, pictures and packing, I couldn't resist following the amazing cold front, to drive 11 hours and climb my favorite tree in a remote chunk of public land in southern Ohio. I didn't arrive at the random and unassuming 3-truck wide parking area in the middle of public land until 3:45am, which gave me a whopping ½ hour to sleep in my truck. However, with decades of experience and success chasing weather motivated bucks on both public and private lands, ½ hour of sleep was all that I needed to provide me with enough rest after a long drive, to complete the 45-minute trek into the forest. Some may think that it is a crazy waste of time and resources to drive 22 hours round-trip for a chance at a mature buck during a 2-day hunt on public land, but those folks just don't have any idea of the level of success that hunting major weather changes has brought to me, readers, viewers, and clients over such a long period of time. The 2016 weather event was a carefully calculated sit opportunity that didn't just offer me the hope of whitetail success, but it offered nearly a guarantee of success. I couldn't wait to sit in my treestand and freeze my toes off during this post-cold front, extremely high value morning sit opportunity!

The wind was just settling down to a manageable level as I approached the final descent into the lower, North-facing elbow shaped narrow ridge that jutted out from a bench system that traveled East to West between two distant clearcuts. As I climbed to an elevation of over 20', the bite of the northwest wind was a welcome addition to the sweaty walk into the stand location. However, as I slowly began to dry out and cool off, the chill of the morning began to creep in. But then it happened! After less than two hours of sit time, a fawn, and then a doe, came running from high above my stand location and down to right alongside the elbow ridge and to my left. A deep grunt then broke through the settling wind gusts and frozen morning! In an instant, the chill was broken and I was about to experience another dose of weather-related mature buck encounters.

My history of broken record, weather-related hunting opportunities, features a collection of whitetail understandings that go well beyond simply shooting a monster buck. If your resources of time and money are precious, and your family enjoys spending a little extra time with you during the hunting season, then understanding the weather forecast can assist you in balancing, not only your hunt, but your hunting season life outside of your favorite treestand. The following pages can deliver a road map of success that extends well beyond your favorite hunting grounds, by helping make sure that you are recognizing and experiencing the best periods of time to head to the woods, in a proven method of dissecting your daily, weekly and monthly high value hunt opportunities. Great hunts like Dante's small private parcel buck, as well as my Ohio public land adventure, are just the tip of the iceberg for the kind of consistent combo of whitetail hunting success and balance, that is waiting for you to capture and enjoy.

Chapter 1

Balanced Whitetail Weather Priorities

Attempting to choose the best day to make sure that my rear-end was in a treestand, began decades ago. The process of forecasting my next hunt was born in an attempt to manage all facets of my life, and not just what would eventually become a portion of my professional whitetail career. Because the resources of both time and money were precious in my life, I needed to make sure that while no day could ever be considered wasted when hunting whitetails, that any day that I actually did choose to hunt, needed to offer the highest level of success that I could ever hope to experience.

What I found as the decades passed was that my system of using the weather to guide my hunting efforts, helped me to minimize the resources of both time and money spent, while actually increasing the rate I connected on mature bucks. Simply, the more years that have passed, the fewer the days that I have needed each season between mature buck encounters.

The practice of forecasting my next hunt has become as much an effort in attempting to manage my family, my career and my hunting grounds, as it has to experience the ultimate level of whitetail harvest success. Best of all, deer forecasting has become a highly proven method for creating consistent target buck encounters on both public and private lands. That is why I am so excited to write, "All Weather Whitetails".

Family

Using the weather to forecast your next buck of a lifetime, can define exactly which days that you should be in the woods and which days that you should be spending time with your family. Whether you have an entire week off or just a weekend, not every day is a great day to hunt. Imagine visiting a corn maze or cider mill with your family instead of forcing a sit during a poor hunting value afternoon. Or how about a football game with your buddies or a cookout, instead of climbing into a stand when the conditions aren't perfect. This is exactly why short, highly defined 2 to 3-day hunts can often yield huge advantages over several day excursions, which often force you to wear out both your family and your hunting grounds during less than ideal weather conditions.

Back in 2005 I had the good fortune of running into a gray faced, fully mature buck that grossed over 170 inches. We called him the Turn Tine buck, and I eventually wrote a whitetail adventure book about the buck. I had actually made the commitment to travel 7 hours South to our hunting grounds in SW WI and stay for about a week; however, there was one huge problem – high temperatures! While sitting during the 3rd day of the hunt in the middle of a hay field catching a sunburn with my good hunting buddy Karl, I made a decision that later paid off significantly. I went home! With daytime highs forecasted in the 70s for a few days, young kids at home and a successful appraisal business waiting for me to attend to, I balanced my priorities of family and work over poor weather conditions.

Returning a few days later, the treestands on the land had been allowed to age like a bottle of fine wine and they were primed for whitetail opportunity, with a significant drop in temperatures. The very first morning of the return trip, Turn Tine came cruising by at a shade before 10am, and the rest is history. Over the years of hunting 7 hours from home, I learned that hunting 1-2 great weather days was worth a week or more of poor weather days, and that translated into not only more time with my family, but more time to focus on my career.

Without being able to use the weather forecast to balance the quality of my time in the field with the priorities of life; including family and friends, I do not believe I would have been able to find the time to pursue my whitetail career.

Career

The best way that I have found to manage any career is by strategically using your time off to slant towards the best days that the weather throws your way. Let's face it, not every hunter can command to experience the best days off to hunt anytime they want. Even as a whitetail professional, I still need to effectively plan my hunting days around a large variety of whitetail work that needs to be completed. I have found no other method of hunting than using the weather to assist me in navigating the balance of my career. In fact, as a hunter in my 20s during the early 90s, I specifically chose banking for a career. The field of banking allowed me to take half days and full days off when I needed to, to make sure that I did not miss the best morning, evening or all-day sit opportunities. And of course, even at a young age I knew about banker's hours and banking holidays! However, I understand that not every hunter has had the luxury of making career choices based on the need for flexible hunting time off.

If you have to beg, borrow or trade to find time to hunt during the season, you are not alone. Even so, that doesn't mean that you have to necessarily sacrifice your level of potential hunting success. Instead, I encourage you to be flexible and consider several potential ways to experience cold weather sits without quitting your job:

*Can you trade a weekend of time off so that you can hunt the 1 perfect weather day during the week?

*Can you find the flexibility for a Monday off instead of a Friday, or visa versa?

*Can you choose 3 weekends off during the rut instead of 1 long week?

*Can you trade an evening off for an early morning off, during the rut?

The trick is to be flexible enough to create opportunities for yourself to not miss 1 or 2 perfect days off, just to be able to experience a long weekend or even an entire week off. Because of work and my hunting partner Karl's choice to live in Georgia, his only option was to drive 21 hours one-way, and then take an entire 9 days off to hunt. On an annual basis during Karl's hunt, we found that he would have 3 to 4 days of great hunting during his 9-day rut hunt - 3 to 4 below average or average days to hunt, and 2 to 3 days that he should just stay inside for the day. Fortunately, Karl had a passion for socializing, playing a little pool, fishing and drinking a little beer, so he actually enjoyed those non-hunting days, and so did Karl's success rate! Karl's bucks often came right after his days off from hunting the land, and he was able to balance his time off to hunt while creating high quality opportunities during his only period of time off. There are several ways that you may find that you can be flexible with your time off from your career, while still maximizing your time in a treestand, even if you aren't a professional in the hunting industry!

Your best treestand location should be the NEXT stand that you shoot your buck of a lifetime out of and not the LAST. Stand and land preservation is key.

Your Hunting Land and Treestands

The activity of burning out your land and treestands, is where a heavy dose of proven hunting strategy can take you a very long way towards all of your whitetail goals! If your desire is to create the best herd and hunt possible, then you have to have patience, and just like your family and career, it doesn't pay to burn out your land and treestands. If you can choose to hunt the best days of the year, or at least be flexible in coming close, then your personal deer forecast will keep you from burning out all of your priorities – whether they be whitetail priorities or not!

The best way to consistently shoot more bucks, is to spend a whole lot more time on the couch. It is no secret that a large percentage of mature buck hunters experience a very low number of days spent in the field per buck kill. Looking back over my top 25 bucks, at least 75% of those bucks were shot using that particular stand or blind, for the first time, for the entire year. While I will leave the entirety of those stats to a later chapter in this book, another critical stat is that I am able to have the option to harvest a 4-year old buck or older, for every 5-7 times I sit, on an annual basis. That stat has only improved over time, including my public land sits. The fact that I exclusively use the weather to forecast my deer hunts has not only kept me from burning out my family, career, land and treestands, but it has significantly raised the number of mature bucks that

I am able to experience per sit. The patience needed to hunt by the weather and creating highly efficient buck opportunities, has combined to prove that you really can shoot more bucks by sitting on the couch.

Conclusion

Do you have to maximize your hunting time while making sure that you keep from burning out your family, career and hunting land? Then using the weather forecast to narrow down the best days to be in the woods, is for you! There are two interesting statements that I often hear from the same hunters at the same time: "I work and I have other priorities, so I can't hunt every day", and "You can't kill them from the couch". Well, guess what? Those two statements go hand-in-hand for creating the potential for whitetail hunting opportunities, because by using the weather you make sure that when you actually do enter the woods to hunt, you can get the most out of your resources of time and money.

Heck, I can hunt just about any day that I want all season long; however, I also create more than 100 videos and articles throughout the season on an annual basis, sometimes finish a book and love spending time with my family and friends. I need to make sure that when I do choose to place my rear-end in a treestand, that I am getting the most out of my time afield, and I bet that you do too.

For nearly 3 decades, the weather has made sure that I can experience the best of the best when it comes to making sure that I don't miss out on the perfect deer hunting days to be in the woods. Consistently creating mature buck hunting opportunities isn't about sitting in a treestand every hour of every chance you get; instead, creating mature buck hunting encounters is about choosing the right days to hunt based on the weather, and then doing your best to not miss out. Less time equals more success when it comes to regularly killing older bucks; and long ago I found that deer forecasting my own hunt greatly assisted me in balancing the true priorities in life, all at the same time.

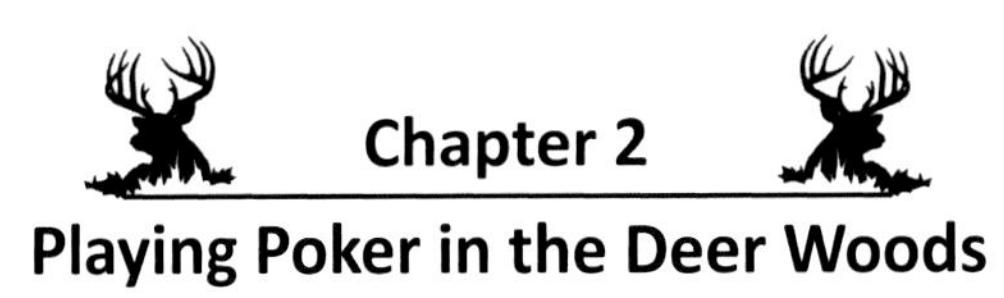

Chapter 2

Playing Poker in the Deer Woods

From 1993 to 2010 I spent 16 out of 17 seasons hunting Pennsylvania's northern public land gun season opener. I hunted with up to 17 hunters at one time; and one of the main things I learned about PA hunting cabin life, was that I was a horrible poker player. I eventually gave up playing at camp in favor of going to bed early, relaxing by the fire with a magazine or strategizing about the next day's hunt. What's interesting about my entire hunting career is that while I have only played enough 10 cent poker to lose $30 or less in a cabin, I have played enough poker in the deer woods to fill my walls with thousands of dollars of deer heads. Following the season's weather fronts is your best bet for a winning hand for whitetails, all season long.

The Game of Odds

I have an extreme passion for hunting whitetails because mature bucks demand a high level of strategy to consistently kill. And I love constantly trying to figure those old monster bucks out! While I have never enjoyed sitting in a chair for hours playing poker at a table, I do understand that knowing when to fold or not, and of course when to play your hand, are both critical strategies that you need to know how to master. And last but not least, the best poker players know the odds of success based on the hands that they are dealt, often to the exact percentage of potential success. I am often amazed at how many hunters constantly play the odds at the cabin poker table, but then dismiss the importance of playing poker in the deer woods. Are you all in – all the time, when you hunt for a monster buck? Well if you are, then those wise old bucks are typically going to empty your pockets during your first few sits, just like my PA hunting buddies did to me. Using the weather to your advantage is like cheating in the deer woods, because you can know the potential odds of your success before ever stepping foot in the woods!

Cheating the Game

While you can potentially win with any hand of weather that you re dealt, I firmly believe that there is a pile of 1% sits and there are only a few 40% sits, lightly scattered throughout the entire season. Knowing exactly which days offer the highest percentage of potential success, can help you weed out the poor value days. Taking a pass on low potential days, keeps you from placing undue levels of hunting pressure on the deer herd, your stands and the land that you hunt. The weather offers a methodical book of hunting success percentages, to assist you in managing your entire sit rotation all season long. One of my favorite whitetail games, is continually analyzing the weather forecast for up to 2 weeks in advance, and then honing-in on only the best days to plan my sits around. When so many hunters burn their stands out on low-potential hunting days, it really does feel like cheating to have a forecasted list of high and low sit values at your disposal. Choosing the best weather values is important for your hunt, but don't forget about the importance of avoiding the pitfalls of hunting low value days.

Playing the game less equals more success in the deer woods, when it comes to consistently placing your tag on an unsuspecting mature buck.

Folding During Low Value Forecast Days

An aspect of low value sit days that is critical to understand, is that there is no number of low value sit days that can add up to, or surpass, a high level sit day. High level sit days are the kings of the calendar and have produced nearly all of my best bow bucks, as well as a portion of my best gun bucks, since the early 90s. However, all of those great weather hunting opportunities would likely have not taken place, regardless of the weather forecast, if I had not managed the high number of poor weather hunting days leading up to them.

Although you most likely do not have the luxury of hunting every great day to be in the woods, you can still play the odds the best that you can by cheating towards the higher potential days. At all costs, I urge you to do your best to avoid hunting your best stand on a very poor day to hunt, such as skipping out of an 82 degree day with 35mph winds on November 3rd in lower MI, in favor of a 57 degree day with 15mph winds just 2 days later. Of course, you can shoot a giant on a poor weather day, but I have experienced that the odds can be heavily tilted in your favor, by patiently waiting for the best odds to combine in the forecast. Reducing the number of low value days that you hunt throughout the entire season, or eliminating them all-together, offers several advantages for your hunt, herd and habitat.

Your entire whitetail strategy, including what you shoot, how many choices that you have to shoot, and the quality of what you have to shoot, can be increased when you decrease the number of poor weather days that you choose to spend in a treestand. Do you want to build a great herd, consistently shoot the best bucks in the neighborhood, and experience outstanding hunts with a deer herd that is focused on your land all season long? Then you can't afford to spook the deer off the land that you hunt and over-pressure the land that you hunt. By making sure that you navigate your hunting season towards the low-pressure, high-reward method of hunting the best weather days, you can keep your intrusions to a minimum and increase your opportunities to a maximum.

Whether you study a 45 day, 10 day or 7 day forecast, there are typically less than 25% of all days that are truly great days to climb into a treestand. Through the influence of the rut, that potential could be raised to include 35% of the forecast during that time of the season; but the bottom line is that there are typically several times more poor to average days to hunt, than great days. Following the weather keeps you off your land and out of your treestands, which allows your sanctuaries to truly be sanctuaries, the local deer herd to experience low pressure habitat on your land, and for the 40% sit opportunities that are in the forecast, to remain at their highest potential.

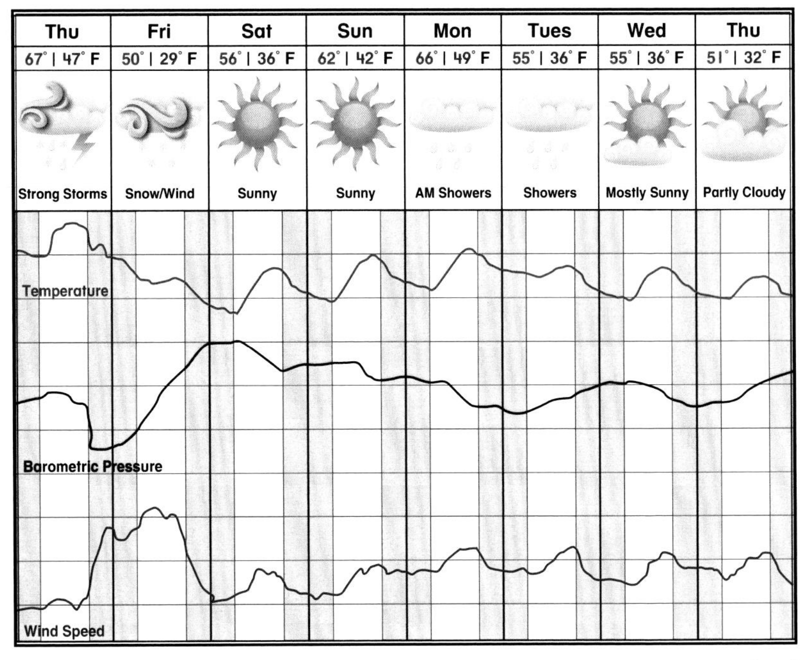

Would you like to unfairly tilt the odds in your favor the next time you head to your favorite treestand? Then make sure to use the tips in this book for allowing the weather forecast to guide you to success.

Going All In

Once you have minimized your number of poor value sits, and have calculated an outstanding day or more to hunt for a monster buck that you are after, it is time to go all-in! These are the days that I begged, borrowed and pleaded for when I worked in banking back in the 90s. These are now the days that I push all of my whitetail work aside, and my family obligations or friends have to wait, because the power of these days to fulfill my whitetail dreams, is undeniable. High value weather sits, command respect. If you can switch a long weekend with a Friday off, to a Monday off instead in order to raise your overall values for the weekend, then go for it! If you can go back to work for a few days during a bad stretch of weather in the middle of a week off, then that's a great idea. If you can trade a weekend off for a prime day during the middle of the week, it will be worth it. Those are just some of the ways to maximize your time in the field, while strategically managing your number of low value sits overall, and at the same time making sure that you can cash in during some of the best days of the entire season!

Conclusion

Do you play a better game of poker in the cabin or in your treestand? This season try making sure that you know when to be patient and fold, and when to attack and go all-in, by following the weather ingredients needed for the best deer forecasted days discussed later in this book. Whether you are a professional hunter and can hunt just about any day that you want to, or you have a 40 hour work week with a level of seniority and have to plan your time off ahead of time, doing your best to play the odds of whitetail weather success will help you build a winning hand this season, as well as every season that follows.

Chapter 3

All Weather Whitetail Stats

There are a couple of types of hunters when it comes to consistently shooting mature bucks with a bow: A specific pattern hunter, and an all-season hunter. Ok, there are a lot more types of hunters besides just those two; however, I think that when it comes to weather, those two really stick out!

The first hunter hunts by using a specific pattern and often a specific treestand to harvest his buck every single year. For example, you may know hunters who annually harvest their buck from roughly the same setup in the first few days of bow season. They rely on early season patterns for bucks that annually slot into the same historical daylight movement as they travel towards the same combination of afternoon food sources, every single year. There are rut hunters as well, that rely on the same cruising stand or two to kill their buck from, just like clockwork. Both types of pattern hunters take advantage of a different set of circumstances to routinely harvest their bucks, but the end result is the same almost every year, and their taxidermist is happy.

As long as a buck is available within their pattern of expertise, a pattern hunter can be highly successful. But what if the patterns change? Timber harvest, neighboring land sales and Ag field rotations can all contribute to ever-changing major daylight deer influences, both good and bad. An all-season whitetail hunter is what I encourage you to become, because like the weather, your hunting approach can be completely fluid, as the rise and fall of hunting season opportunity comes your way. Are you an early season hunter, an October lull hunter, a Pre Rut hunter, a rut hunter, a gun hunter or a late season hunter? How about becoming an all-season whitetail hunter, so that you can take advantage of great deer movements and the perfect big buck days, over the course of an entire season.

After a 40 degree temperature drop and an incredible wind speed reduction, it was worth the 700 mile drive to hunt two days for this 2016 Ohio public land archery buck.

All Weather Whitetail Stats

My personal hunting stats reflect that if I had relied on only one or two buck patterns to hunt over the course of an entire season, I would have killed a lot fewer bucks! By learning to recognize the high value days at any time during the season, you can develop a hunting method that allows you the flexibility to jump in and hunt every facet of the season during the best days that portion of the season has to offer. During the hunting season, spending more time on the couch, more time with family and friends and more time on the whitetail priorities of my life outside of hunting, has directly enhanced my level of success from the treestand, all season long.

Hunting high value days has been so incredibly and predictably successful. Instead of hunting a specific pattern, I choose to hunt the best days that feature the greatest potential of deer movement first, and then match that day to whatever pattern the deer are currently using. Based on trail cameras, scrape and rub sign, if I have a buck within a certain pattern, I wait for a high value day and hunt him ASAP. It doesn't matter what time of the season it is, the combination of current mature buck movement and a great weather day can't be missed, because both are fleeting. Here are some random stats relating to my own personal buck hunting history:

* My top 25 bucks from MI, PA and Ohio public lands, as well as from both MI and WI private lands, have been shot between October 12th and the end of December.

* My 3rd best archery buck was shot the 9th and final day of WI's 2015 Gun season.

* My 1st and 2nd best archery bucks were shot on October 22nd and November 8th, respectively.

* My top 10 gun season bucks in the states of WI, MI and PA, have been shot on the first day of gun season, the 3rd day, 4th day, 7th day, 9th day and 15th day.

* Out of my top 50 bucks, I've used 47 different stand or blind locations.

*Out of my top 50 bucks, at least 45 have been shot using that particular blind or treestand for the first time that season.

While my buck harvests appear random, with the exception of 1 opening day gun season buck out of 3, over 20 bucks out of my top 25 (more bow than gun) were shot on high value days going back over 2 decades. Again, "if I have a buck within a certain pattern, I wait for a high value day and hunt him ASAP". That applies to every portion of the season that I still have a tag to hunt with.

It doesn't matter what time of the year it is, I have an extreme passion for hunting specific target bucks that are currently active, and then going in for the kill using whatever fresh stand location is available. The stand locations that I use are fresh because I have specifically passed on poor weather days, in favor of hunting great weather days. Due to hunting small private parcels and public land, I just can't afford to burn out my stands, which in turn burns out the lands that I hunt.

As I mentioned in my last whitetail strategy book, Mature Buck Success by Design, your favorite stand should be the next stand that you shoot your buck out of, and not your last. It pays to have a short memory. Taking an all-season, fluid and opportunistic approach dictated by hunting current buck sign, and using the weather to narrow down exactly which days to hunt, is the only method that I have found to consistently harvest mature bucks on an annual basis – no matter what time of the season it is! Don't be surprised if after a few decades, your own all-season buck stats become as random as the variety of stand locations that you choose to hunt your bucks from.

It's no surprise that some of my favorite trail cam photos have been captured during the same weather patterns that I have a passion for hunting - cold clearing skies and dying winds.

Conclusion

If the land changes, the timber is cut, the Ag field plantings are rotated, your hunting grounds turn into a subdivision, or you lose your favorite lease, using the weather to help you capitalize on all-season opportunities, can navigate you to consistent whitetail success no matter when the opportunity presents itself. If you enjoy being a pattern hunter for a specific portion of the season out of a particular stand or two, the power of the weather forecast can guide you to an incredible level of success by knowing exactly which day to go in for the kill. I personally enjoy being an All Weather Whitetail hunter, all-season long. No matter which portion of the season you choose to head to a treestand, you can use the wind, rain, snow, heat and cold to pinpoint exactly when to capture your own 40% sit opportunities, while creating your own lifetime of random hunting stats.

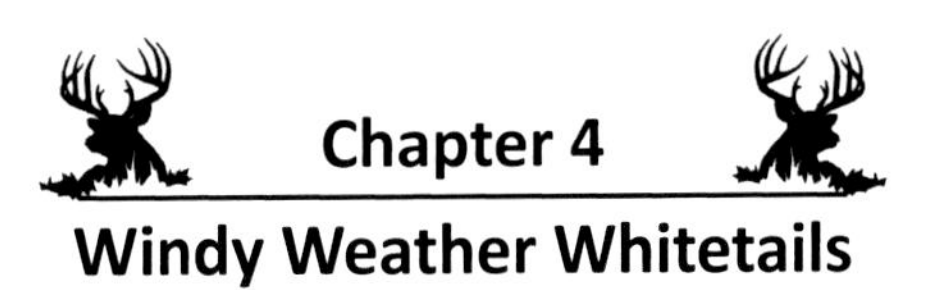

Chapter 4

Windy Weather Whitetails

The date was October 26th, 2007, and my buddy Joe and I had just driven down to hunt the backside of a cold front the night before, right in the middle of the SW WI Pre Rut. With a temperature drop of over 30 degrees and a rising barometric pressure, the weather had aligned to usher out several days of high temperatures, heavy rain and winds. The only potential problem was that the wind was still hanging on. What that meant was that I had to find a stand position that allowed me to take advantage of shelter – shelter for both myself and the local deer herd.

My hunting focus was lasered in on a giant 15-point buck that I had first caught glimpse of on the last day of the 2006 bow season. I knew he was in the area, and there was only one treestand that fit the conditions for a heavy Northwest wind, Pre Rut morning hunt. As I made my way along the difficult, side-hill 45-minute trek towards the stand location, I could hear the trees blowing high above along the ridgeline, as well as trees blowing on the exposed, Northerly facing slope across the deep hollow. Not even a leaf stirred as I approached my stand, and I was banking the local deer herd, appreciating the calm, lee side of the hollow. It wasn't until 4 hours later that I would find out if my bet would pay off.

Wind Stress

I know it will be a broken record in this book going forward, but deer feed 5 times in a 24-hour period as rhythmic pattern feeders. No different than a baby that wakes us up every 2-3 hours with cries to feed them, deer experience those same, set, feeding patterns. When winds blow hard with branches breaking and trees dancing in every direction, deer can become completely stressed – stressed enough to miss out on not only quality feedings in open Ag lands or hardwoods, but entire feedings all-together. The wind helps to set the table for not only a roller coaster of feeding cycle opportunities, but spikes in deer movement as well. Always remember that stressed deer become hungry deer, and hungry deer eventually become moving deer. Whether it's wind, rain, snow or cold, deer movements can drastically increase, often parallel in intensity to the severity of the weather.

Wind Matters

A PA deer study a few years ago revealed that deer movements actually picked up a little when wind speeds increased. Unfortunately, hunters grasped at that tidbit of information to hunt excessive winds in potentially grave treestand situations, with the wind howling and compound bows swaying in the wind. Social media was alive with hunters urging other hunters to hunt on high wind days. I couldn't help but picture a hunter on a remote, wooded point far above the hollow below, hugging a giant old oak for his dear life, as the winds pummeled him from the Northwest. Could you shoot a giant buck during high winds? Sure, just like you have the potential to shoot a mature buck during extreme heat, blizzards and thunderstorms. I call those 1% sits, because, while it could happen, it isn't very likely. However, that doesn't mean that extreme weather does not offer hunting opportunity. Extreme wind offers some great opportunities to hit the deer woods, if you follow these 5 simple rules:

1. Wind Speed Change is Key

While a 30mph wind is a very stiff breeze, it pales in comparison to a 50mph wind. Likewise, a 10mph is a stark contrast compared to a 30mph wind. It's all relative. When the wind significantly diminishes, it is time to hit the woods! My favorite wind forecasts are those that allow you to sneak into a stand location with heavy winds to mask your intrusion, followed by a sharp decrease in wind speed.

2. Lee Side Opportunities

Everyone thinks about the lee side of a ridgeline, but what about the quiet side of a stand of evergreens, an expansive block of hardwoods, a large clearcut, or a thick, pure stand of switchgrass? What I have experienced is that during major winds, deer gravitate to the much calmer, downwind edges of cover – hills or no hills.

3. Steady Wind is Your Friend

The hunt described in the intro of this chapter, involved a treestand setup that was ¾ of the way up in elevation, above the ravine below. With steady winds above during the morning hours, I could count on thermals that would carry my scent above my position, well into afternoon hours. While evening thermals settle typically only during the last 30 to 45 minutes of daylight, morning thermals can continue to rise for several hours, making a morning stand location that is above the expected line of travel, ideal for your ambush.

4. Reliable Moderate Evening Winds

When hunting in hill country, you can count on evening thermals to carry your scent below, even if that thermal is sometimes the complete opposite of the forecasted wind direction. However, once wind speeds reach 8-12mph or greater, you can often find that the wind speed is great enough to fight off the effects of evening thermals.

5. Wind Equals Deer Movement

Sure, I believe that extreme wind patterns cause deer to increase movements; however, I do not believe that means in any way, that deer move more within their typical daily patterns. Instead, when and if deer move more in moderate to heavy winds, I have experienced that they are doing so to find shelter. Can you imagine what happens when you combine a high percentage of the deer herd during the rut, within the same, hidden and quieter portion of the habitat? That is why the lee side of hills or cover, can be the magic ticket towards a mature buck that you are after this season.

Waiting for the wind to significantly decrease is an outstanding tactic. However, heading to the lee side of a ridge system during a period of heavy winds can often place you in the middle of a high percentage of the local deer herd, choosing to take shelter within a small percentage of the local habitat.

Wind Forecast Reliability

There are several online forecasts that feature an hour by hour forecast of wind direction and speed. Of course, those same forecasts often feature barometric pressure, moisture probability percentage, precipitation type and amount, etc. When it comes to the wind forecasts, though, you can expect an accurate reflection of what is going to happen on the hour for up to 3 days in advance. In fact, I find that wind speed and wind direction is the most accurate portion of the 72-hour forecast. Combining high value hunting days with a 72-hour plan of attack including precise wind directions and wind speeds, are some pretty deadly ingredients that you can use to hone in on a specific target buck that you are after!

Conclusion

Little did I know that upon reaching my treestand on that fateful day in October of 2006, that the buck I was after was getting his picture taken150 yards above me at the waterhole. It was well before first light, and even with moderate winds, deer don't typically mind being out in the open during darkness, and he was no exception! If I had taken the easy way in to the stand across the open fields, I would have surely spooked him away for good. Around 10am Joe and I checked in by cell phone to confirm that neither of us had seen any deer, but by 10:15 the mature, 15 point was lying dead in the quiet ravine far below, as the trees still danced in the wind against the blue sky above. He had chosen the lee side of the ridge to chase a doe and fawn across the windless habitat right under my stand location.

Whether it's morning steadily rising thermals, the lee side of hills or cover, severe decreases in the wind speed or a wind-induced feeding spike by a stressed-out and hungry deer herd, the wind is your friend when it comes to whitetails. While that doesn't mean that the odds are on your side for sitting in your favorite treestand while being assaulted by 50mph winds, it does mean that heavy winds do create whitetail opportunities all season long. When you combine extreme wind and the high value days discussed later in this book, you can experience some of the best deer days that the annual whitetail season has to offer.

Chapter 5

Extreme Rain Deer Hunting Tactics

The rain continued to fall hard as it masked my approach to the bowstand. I had entered the edge of the field 2 hours after daybreak so that I could survey the entire field from a slight ridge and make sure that the coast was clear. I continued directly to the stand location with the wind at my back, allowing my scent to be carried well above the hollow below. I approached the stand from a higher elevation and settled into my treestand. I faced slightly to my right and up-hill, with a flat of oaks within 40 yards off my left knee. The rain continued to fall - steady, hard and loud. Not a creature stirred.

I felt like I had been able to enter the stand completely undetected, and I was hoping the giant "Turkey Foot" buck was bedded on the opposite side of the oak flat, tucked into a long bench that extended back behind my left shoulder across the hollow. Experience taught me that a rising full moon in the evening might dictate a quality feeding opportunity during the late morning. The heavy rain was forecasted to stop by 10 am, and the radar supported that, potentially creating a great window of opportunity for an encounter with the old monster buck. Sometime after 11am I could see the huge base of antlers on top of a deer's head as it lazily munched up and down, feeding on acorns as he traveled slowly through the prickly ash. He was coming! Hunting a hole in the rain was about to pay off, if I did my part.

Rainy Deer Perspective

Of course, we can only guess what goes through a whitetail's brain during any event in its life; however, when the rain is hammering the forest floor it isn't that hard to imagine. The blurry, loud and unrelenting pounding of a thunderstorm has got to be a major source of stress to a deer herd. Have you heard that deer feed 5 times in a 24-hour period as rhythmic pattern feeders? I apologize for repeating that last statement from chapter 4, but I have a feeling that you will read it again in this book because it is so important, as it relates to the foundation of advanced whitetail strategies. Stress, cold temps and missed quality feedings all add together to equal 1 giant hunger pain in a deer's belly. Whether it is cold weather, high winds, excessive snow or unrelenting rain, you can take advantage of the extremity of weather when it comes to filling your tag. From a deer's perspective rain is a common occurrence, but there are several uncommon strategies caused by wet weather that you can plan a great hunt around.

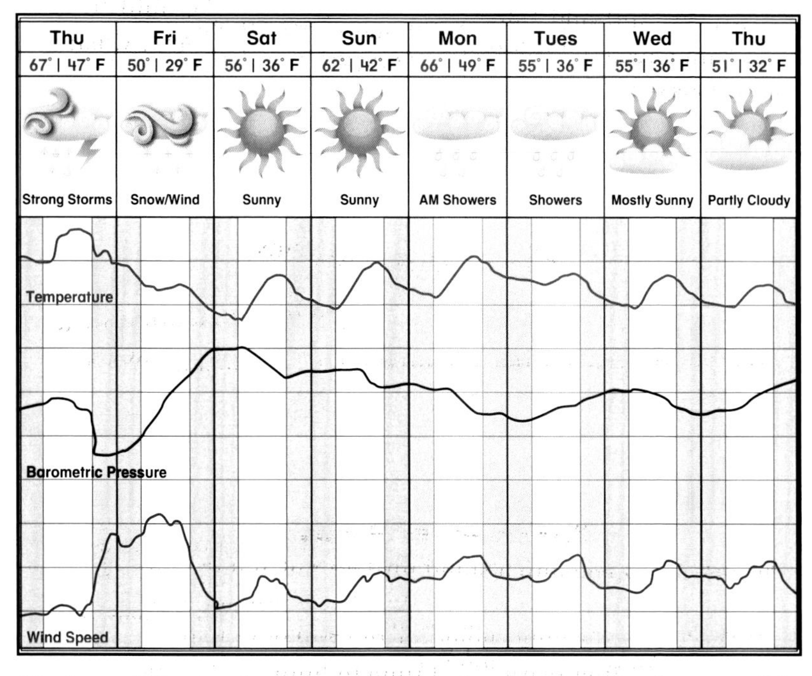

The hours following the end of pounding thunderstorms can be some of the best periods of time to hunt whitetails that are on the move. However, make sure to take note of significant holes of 3 to 4 hours or more between the showers.

Rain Matters

If you have a monster buck you are after, he doesn't leave the forest just because there is pouring rain. He is available for harvest; but during extreme rain events it is very hard to do so because he often doesn't move. Tracking him can be difficult even if you do get a shot off, but the odds of a whitetail moving in the driving rain are very poor in the first place. However, there are 5 rainy weather strategies that you can practice, to help you bring home the venison:

1. Rainy Weather Approach

Your ability to access your stand location is significantly enhanced when the woods are full of moisture and the sounds of the weather. Wet vegetation and various noises caused by wind and rain, can allow you to sneak into the woods undetected. Prolonged showers can also quickly wash away your scent. During a major rainstorm, you cannot only access your stand locations undetected, but you can access at a time when the majority of the local whitetail herd is pinned down in their bedding areas.

2. Extreme Thunderstorms

The worst thunderstorms create the best opportunities for deer movement. I have experienced that the longer the storm rages on, the greater the potential for deer movement when the storm finally breaks. The effects of continued excessive noise, lack of vision and missed feeding opportunities are magnified when the storm just won't quit.

3. Holes in The Showers

Of course slipping into a stand undetected and then waiting for skies to clear is one outstanding strategy, but don't overlook major, gaping holes in the radar in-between the showers. An often-overlooked time to hunt is when there is enough time between showers that the drips from the leaves, branches and treestands dry up. This is the calm between the storms. By studying radar enough, you can guesstimate the time it will take for one shower to end and for the next one to begin. When the time in-between is at least 2 hours or more, try taking advantage of stealthy access for both entering and exiting your stand locations. This may set up perfectly for a quality early morning or late afternoon hunt, but don't forget about slipping into a stand that covers a small hunting plot, an apple tree or a stand of oaks adjacent to a bedding area. A quality hunt between rain showers on a remote food source right next to a bedding area, can potentially offer an outstanding 2-3 hour hunt out of an otherwise low value day. It sure did for me in 2010 with the "Turkey Foot" buck.

4. Quiet Stealth

During wet weather back in the mid 80s, my brother and I were just a couple of teenagers with bows in our hand and a whole lot more confidence than hunting experience or skill. However, we were able to follow the tracks of a big 8 point right to the big 8 point! The 8-point stood up on a knoll in the oaks and stared at us in surprise, and we did the same. We never came close to releasing an arrow (again zero experience or skill), but that encounter was due to the wet and damp soggy weather that allowed us to move through the woods undetected. I later found that same buck dead after he had been shot and unrecovered in the chunk of Pontiac State Recreation area of lower MI that we had been hunting. He was an outstanding 3-year old buck that would have been a great buck now from the area, let alone then. I used his antlers as rattling antlers into the late 2000's, until someone stole them from my shed in the UP of MI.

5. Northwest Cold Fronts

A Southwest wind warm front that clears out a rainy weather event, also offers a decent time to hunt within 24 hours after the storm clears. However, when the winds turn from the Northwest and signal a major temperature drop – do everything in your power to hit your favorite treestand for a NW wind! A forecasted Northwest wind on the backside of a front, is exactly the same variety of front that delivered to me the 15-point buck described in Chapter 4. Northwest winds are the winds of change during the hunting season, signifying cold temperatures, first frosts, snow and an overall decrease in temperatures. In fact, a November 10th, 1975 storm with hellacious NW winds is responsible for taking the Edman Fitzgerald down in Lake Superior. The entire crew of 29 was lost. While Northwest winds are typically NOT the predominant winds, as illustrated by numerous historical wind graphs found online for the months of October, November and December, they are the winds of change, the strongest winds; and in my experience, they have accounted for over ½ of all of my mature buck harvests. When the Northwest winds blow on the backside of rainy weather - or snow for that matter - it is time to pay attention to the opportunities that they represent!

Rainy Radar Forecast

As a word of caution, it is important to read or listen to the weather forecast to establish a base of what might happen on a given day, and then learn to watch the weather for yourself. The radar doesn't lie. It is pretty easy to forecast for yourself by watching the radar to determine whether the approaching rain is slamming into dry air and dissipating, or if it is jumping into warm, moist air and expanding. Most of the online radar sources offer the radar in 15 to 20-minute intervals or less so that you can guesstimate the track of the storm and approximate timing of the storm, for several hours prior to when it will hit. Becoming an amateur meteorologist isn't a bad idea when aspiring to be an All Weather Whitetail hunter!

Driving rains can significantly suppress deer movement. This creates and outstanding opportunity to access your favorite treestand completely undetected; right before the rain lets up and deer become active.

Conclusion

The 2010 "Turkey Foot" buck was part of an ideal rainy weather hunt. Steady, heavy rain allowed for an undetected approach and climb into the stand, and the break in the weather created an immediate feeding opportunity on an oak flat adjacent to a mature buck bedding area. Enough time had passed for the woods to dry out to create a late morning, moon and weather induced feeding spike that successfully set the table for an outstanding October 22nd opportunity. The only problem? The nimrod behind the bow! A small twig steered the arrow from success to failure. The best part of the story is that my hunting partner Karl, was able to take advantage of the missed opportunity by harvesting the buck during a morning cold front sit, just 10 days later. Kill or not, the rain induced encounter is one of my most exciting hunts to this day, and a testament to what wet weather can offer during an otherwise washed-out day.

Chapter 6

Flurries to Blizzards for Mature Bucks

The sudden noise from the muzzleloader screamed across the Ag field ridgetop before bouncing between the snow-covered hardwood points behind the magnificent 6-year old 8 point. The wide 8 ran to my right, sprinting closer and closer to the edge of the CRP field. He then stopped in the several inches of snow, and the frantic panic began. The smoke from the shot hadn't even cleared the air as it drifted like a fog to the Southeast. I desperately attempted to reload my muzzleloader. The giant buck stood still at 125 yards, looking for the noise that spooked his feeding time. Finally, loaded! But then it happened - I couldn't pull the spent 209 primer out of the breech! I ripped my fingernails back trying to pull the primer, as blood dripped down the back of the barrel and eventually into the snow below. Looking back to that fateful 2010 hunt and the snowstorm that served to set it up, it is pretty easy to recognize that particular snowy weather hunt as my most memorable cold weather hunt since 1986! And I've had a lot of them.

When hunting season cold fronts turn from rain into snow, you can bet that some prime-time mature buck opportunities are going to take place. While I have had a passion for hunting any Fall cold front, going back decades, there is something special when snow, below freezing temperatures and hard frosts combine. What can add to the excitement of a snow-filled cold front, is that as a Midwest hunter to the core, the timing of these super fronts typically takes place right during the annual whitetail rut.

Prime Time Cold Fronts

While a snow front potentially carries the same values as any other hunting season cold front, the importance can be magnified because the first flurries of the Winter often fall during the annual whitetail rut. Snow obviously means cold, but it also reveals a magical time of whitetail movement and deer activity during the hunting season.

When I ran beagles for both hunting and field trials, there was nothing better than a few inches of wet snow for incredible scenting conditions. The snow seemed to act as a sponge for holding scent. I've witnessed fawns dancing around a mock scrape, with nothing more than the collection of natural gland scent covering the end of the vine. I've witnessed the same with fawns during the season's first snows. Are they excited by the first snow? The collection of scent? Who knows why deer seem to go nuts with the first flakes of the year, but when the whitetail rut and the first snow falls combine, they can infuse the annual hunting season's prime time to create monster buck opportunities!

Following periods of frozen snow and single digit temperatures, make sure to be in your favorite treestand near a browse filled bedding area when temperatures climb above freezing.

Snow Matters

Throughout the decades I've had the pleasure of hunting during multiple blizzard events, and with the exception of a few UP of Michigan migration movements, the pickings have been slim to none when hunting some of the hunting season's worst weather events. The great thing is that while extreme snow conditions can bring the local deer movement to a standstill at one moment, they can significantly increase deer activity on the other end of the scale. Here are 5 snowy weather factors that you can use to plan some extremely high value sits, in particular when they fall during the annual whitetail rut:

1. Front Side Feeding Opportunity

An approaching snowstorm is no surprise. The media causes a rush on bread, milk, eggs, candles and flashlights even if the "storm" only ends up producing an inch or less of the white stuff. Somehow I believe that whitetails can pick up on the news outlets, because there are times that every deer in the neighborhood is out in the fields before a snowstorm, packing away the groceries. 12-24 hours before the Northwest winds attack the landscape with 3' snowdrifts and frozen fence posts, the lite Easterly winds bring clouds and slowly falling temperatures to a deer population that is often heavily feeding. They have picked up on the falling barometric pressure – nature's weather forecast! Finding a hidden oak flat, cluster of apples, or a back corner of a food plot can be the perfect spot to find an old brute that has chosen to fill his belly before the full force of the storm hits. This is where the east wind treestands that you thought you would never use, can pay-off in a big way!

2. Mid Storm Wet and Calm

At some point after the Easterly winds have begun to usher in wet snow, and before the Northwest winds have taken over to bring rapidly falling temperatures and heavy snowfall rates per hour, there is often a calming period as the snow storm spins and re-adjusts to allow the cold front to come slamming through. You can often discover the hole in the radar, and it is fairly easy to time your opportunity just right. If this period of time falls during the morning to mid-day hours, seek a stand, observing daytime browse or natural food sources directly adjacent to a bedding area. If the opening in the radar falls during the afternoon hours, don't hesitate to sit somewhat invasively over a high quality afternoon food source, with the knowledge that deer will soon be pushed back into their bedding hours to facilitate a non-invasive, windy, wet and snowy retreat from your stand location.

3. Protection Movements

During the 2010 hunt for the huge 8 point that I referenced during the intro, I began the hunt by traveling through heavy snow fall and wading through 8-10 inches of fresh snow. The weather was forecasted to blow through within an hour, leaving me with a 3 to 4-hour sit facing into diminishing Northwest winds, clearing skies and significantly dropping temperatures prior to dark. Then it happened! During the middle of the sit and still 2-3 hours prior to dark, deer began filing out of the hollow facing to the Northwest, through the saddle in the middle of the CRP field, heading over, down and into the more protected hollow to the Southeast. I still remember that prior to the Wide 8 showing up last, I had watched 43 deer make the crossing. 43 deer during 1 sit is still my #1 sit for deer numbers ever in SW WI, going all the way back to the season of 2002. When deer become trapped and exposed during a major snow storm, make sure to place yourself between their current location and where they will temporarily reside once the storm blows through.

4. Evening Feeding Explosion

The first and second evenings after the storm blows through, the temperatures should be cold, the conditions calm and the high quality food sources full of extremely hungry whitetails. During a major storm you can expect whitetails to miss up to 5 important feedings during a 24-36 hour period. Feedings #1 and #2 take place during the morning and early afternoon time slots, feeding #3 takes place in their highly preferred afternoon pre-dark food source, and feedings #4 and #5 take place in safe, social open locations where deer are fairly protected and have plenty of average quality food to dine on. When a major snow storm takes place, the higher volume, high quality feedings during #3, #4 and #5 time slots, are often completely missed. Deer are forced to stay in their bedding areas or even worse, move to conifer or grass pockets that offer zero feeding opportunities, in favor of thermal protection. Missed quality feedings, stress and extreme cold complete the triad of energy robbing conditions that set the table for heavy feeding as soon as the conditions moderate. Placing yourself on a high quality food source or on the way to an afternoon food source, can place the oldest buck in the neighborhood right in your lap.

5. Post Storm Warm-ups

Frozen hard and squeaky snow can grip a region for days at a time, but eventually the below freezing daily temperatures change to morning fog and temperatures in the high 30s and 40s. This is a time when I love to hunt on the back side of browse filled bedding areas during a morning hunt. When conditions are frozen, deer are often bedded during the coldest portion of the day, which is at daybreak. However, when conditions turn soft with melting snow, a morning hunt can be a great option. This condition often takes place during early December at a time when the Secondary Rut is taking place. I recommend that you use an access that brings you into the stand location by taking the long way around the land, and well away from major morning feeding locations. This is also a great time for mid-day and afternoon sits, and I like to place a preference on remote funnel hotspots of mock scrapes and waterholes on the way to an afternoon food source.

Morning Bedding Opportunities

My step son Dante and I had an exceptional morning hunt back in 2014 during an early December Sunday. After a storm had blanketed the area with snow two days prior to the hunt, we chose to hunt a morning stand in a remote location, taking advantage of an unharvested soybean movement that was planted over a ½ mile away. We had a great early morning sit, with a line of deer filing by just after daybreak. The nice 4-year old 10 point in the group didn't offer a shot for Dante, and for the next few hours we waited with no other deer sightings.

As the temperatures increased into the 30s and then 40s towards lunchtime, we made a bad decision to go watch a portion of the Detroit Lions game. Not a bad decision in that the Lions typically lose - actually won that day- but a bad decision in that by the time we got back to the stand 3 hours before dark, the 10-point was with the same group of deer, within bowshot of our treestand! The deer bounded away and we missed a golden opportunity for a very nice buck, a buck that had likely chosen to leave his bedding area and browse during a mid-day snow melt. This hunt reinforced the priority of hunting the melting snow following a period of frozen conditions, in particular during the middle of the day near bedding areas. I have found that the morning hours are more of a gamble during frozen conditions because you just can't be certain if a buck is already in his bedding area or not, when you are approaching your treestand. Although Dante and I would have missed the Lions game, we would have placed ourselves in a much better timing position by letting the deer go to bed at daybreak, and then following increasing temperatures into our treestand during the middle of the morning.

Small pockets of switchgrass totaling 1/4 acre to 1/2 acre in size, can be the perfect snow-busting thermal bedding compliment to adjacent woody browse, including: hardwood regeneration, woody shrub tips and briars.

Conclusion

Hunting cold fronts and the predictable level of success that has followed, created the foundation of passion and experience to write this book. However, the snow-filled cold fronts of November have created some of my fondest memories going all the way back to 1986, when hunting on a treestand meant standing on a branch that my brother and I would typically climb up to, while holding our bows with frozen fingers.

How fitting then, that my hunt for the Wide 8 in 2010, resulted in numb, bloody fingers. I never was able to remove the 209 primer and finish the reloading process. Of course, I had already missed the giant buck with my muzzleloader at 75 yards broadside, so I can never truly complain, but that afternoon hunt was an incredible snow-filled opportunity that illustrates what can happen when high value snow sits take place.

Chapter 7

Overheated Whitetails Solutions

When the whitetail woods heat up, I typically opt for spending time with family, friends and career. Some of the lowest value days of the year revolve around the highest temperature days of the season. What I have consistently experienced is that although deer still may travel, feed and breed the same amount during a 24-hour period, they do so to a much higher degree under the cover of darkness. However, there is always a silver lining of opportunity when it comes to hunting whitetails during extreme weather patterns, and extreme heat is no exception.

What's great about extreme heat during any time of the season is that the longer the heat persists, the greater the potential of opportunity when a cold front eventually comes barreling through the area. But that's not all! High temperatures also represent a low value consistency that seizes a large portion of the daylight hours. That consistency allows you to capture high value opportunities by using several high heat hunting strategies that help you use unseasonably warm weather forecasts to your advantage.

Above or below average temperatures during the Peak Rut and waterholes can combine to create a deadly combination for long range cruising mature bucks.

Over-heated Deer Herds

While high temperatures and maximum daytime deer movement do not typically coincide, there are still several high heat, deer-related hunting concepts that do! In my experience, shrinking daylight travel routes and a premium placed on soft mass, waterholes and food plot greens, can together lay the foundation for high value hunting opportunities aimed to help you target a deer herd that is heat stressed and thirsty. The consistency of prolonged daytime heat allows you to specifically narrow down your efforts for a suppressed deer herd that will present on a daily basis, a small number of highly defined windows of potential shot opportunities. If you have treestands that relate to full waterholes, bountiful soft mass, cool bedding areas and moisture laden food plot greens, you are in luck!

Extreme Heat Matters

Nasty blizzards, excessive rainstorms, and gale-force winds all create extreme weather deer hunting opportunities, and extreme heat waves are no exception. Although my overall strategy is to avoid heat waves in favor of cooler opportunities, there are times, such as the peak of the rut or during gun season openers, that you can't help but hunt in the heat. Fortunately, there are 5 important extreme heat whitetail strategies that you can focus on to turn poor value days into targeted high purpose sits:

1. Waterholes

Enough positive attributes can't be said when it comes to the opportunities created by water when the habitat heat switch is turned to "High". Small, hidden container or machine dug waterholes that hold a few hundred gallons or less, can be the perfect attraction for thirsty whitetails while they are on their way to their afternoon food sources or near their dry bedding areas. Shade covered waterholes are even better! Cruising bucks between doe bedding areas, near their own bedding areas or on the way to their favorite shaded, afternoon food sources, can be drawn to water like steel to a magnet. Small waterholes can typically be significantly more attractive than large exposed water sources or ponds most of the hunting season, but when hidden micro water sources of 80-500 gallons are available within dry habitats, they can be as attractive as any other whitetail hotspot in the neighborhood. Early morning, mid-day, and an hour or less before sunset, can command the attention of mature bucks, in particular the closer to their bedding areas that they are located.

2. Shady Food Plot Corners

Attempting a morning food plot sit during times of heat is risky at best. Whitetails are either already there feeding and carry a high potential to be spooked when entering a stand, or have already entered their bedding areas and will not be coming back until right before dark. However, the shaded corners of hidden green food sources can feature a high level of attraction for an overheated old monster buck during an afternoon sit. By adding a waterhole on the way to a sun-protected corner and a few soft mass trees, you can create the perfect habitat combination for sun-proofing a specific daily afternoon deer movement.

Moisture filled soft mast can be the perfect solution for thirsty whitetails. Make sure that your mast trees are adjacent to both stands and not too deep in your woods, so that deer have to leave their cover to take a drink from the succulent fruit.

3. Remote Soft Mass

I don't know about you, but the last thing that I want to eat when I'm coming off the land from hanging a stand in 85-degree heat, is a bag chips, a handful of peanuts or some salty crackers. I can't imagine that it is any different than what a deer goes through during a day of high heat. Soft mass equals high moisture content – moisture that deer can process no differently than taking a drink of water. Low moisture content corn, acorns, beans or browse, has to rate pretty low on the preference scale when the going gets hot, compared to crabapples, plums, pears, persimmons or apples. One of the most scrape-ravaged locations in the woods is often a remote cluster of apple trees adjacent to a buck bedding area. Hanging a stand nearby and waiting for a mature buck to poke his head out for a quick "drink" from a few high-moisture content apples, is an outstanding tactic for heat wave hunting conditions. Also, adding a cluster of apples or other soft mass trees to a remote corner of a food plot, adjacent to a shaded approach corridor, can be a great idea for targeting an overheated and wary, shade-loving monster buck.

4. Cool Bedding Area Hotspots

Steep, creek-filled draws, early season shaded hardwood knolls, and seasonably damp conifer swamps can each draw their fair share of whitetails, depending on the time of season that excessive heat waves occur. It isn't uncommon for bucks that are typically bedding in sun exposed semi-open habitat, such as switchgrass, corn or CRP fields, to move to find shade-favorable forms of habitat. A mature buck is likely to beat you to his preferred variety of shaded bedding area well before the hot sun breaks the horizon; however, a remote, heat-protected bedding area can create an exceptional hunt for the individual who is positioned for an afternoon sit and waiting for a late afternoon giant to exit his bedding area.

5. Food Plot Greens

In my experience, not only can high moisture content, hidden and unpressured Fall food plot greens stave off the effects of massive acorn crops, standing corn and unpicked beans, they can also provide just what a heat-oppressed old buck needs: Water! High moisture content food plot varieties such as forage peas, late planted soybeans, rape, turnip, radish, clover, and young oats, rye or wheat, can offer enough moisture for thirsty whitetails, that they don't even need to find standing water. Try giving deer a drink through what they eat, and you can find that not only can you attract, hold and protect a herd that you are trying to build, but you can hunt that herd during a heat wave at the same time.

Heat Wave Morning Forecast Opportunities

During moderate warm-ups and heat waves during the Pre Rut, peak and Post Rut phases, one of the most overlooked heat wave opportunities is the morning hunt. I believe evening hunts are often forced, as hunters gravitate towards defined afternoon whitetail food source movements. Trail cameras tell hunters that mature bucks are still hitting the open habitat food sources, mock scrapes or waterholes during the night, but the heat wave reality check is that those same bucks most likely won't show up in the heat during daylight hours. This is an outstanding time to compare morning to morning lows, instead of the consistently hot, daytime to daytime highs.

The morning forecasted low for any given day, is always the forecast for the next morning's low. For example, if Friday's high is forecasted for 72, and Friday's low is forecasted for 49, 49 is actually Saturday morning's forecasted low temperature. Even if the daytime high temperature forecast is the same for every day, there will still typically be fluctuations in humidity, wind speeds, moisture and cloud cover. What this often creates is a morning low forecast fluctuation any time daytime highs are constant, whether there are cold temps, moderate, or hot temps in the forecast. Make sure not to miss morning temp drops of 5 degrees or more during the rut, even during an extreme heat wave, and especially if the morning forecast is combined with a rising barometric pressure.

A slight morning temp drop and a rising barometric pressure, is an outstanding time to head for a high value sit opportunity near both buck and doe bedding areas. Add a waterhole or a cluster of soft mass trees into the mix, and it's time to sit back and enjoy a high potential, high-heat, mature buck, morning harvest opportunity!

The Heat Wave Setup

Before you can experience high value cold front hunting opportunities, a stable temperature base of several days must take place first. The best hunting ingredient that can originate from an extreme heat wave of several days or more, is when a giant cold front comes smashing through to completely remove and replace the heat. Regardless of waterholes, soft mass clusters, afternoon shaded food plot corners, cool bedding areas or green food sources, the value of a cold front that follows a mega heat wave, can't be competed with.

Conclusion

You can still find whitetail success during sweaty days if you match your hunting strategy to the specific opportunity that the time of the day or time of the season, is presenting. Focusing on a whitetail's thirst, its need for bedding protection, and its short, highly specific movements during the cool of the day can lead you to a high value encounter, even during the worst of heat waves. However, if you have to make a choice over hunting during the heat or waiting and hunting during what comes after the heat, your choice should always be an easy one: Be patient my friend!

Chapter 8

Long Range Deer Forecasting Opportunities

In this next chapter I get right to the point of how to read the weather forecast so that you can experience a lifetime of high value sits on your own. For nearly 30 years I have enjoyed the process of using the weather forecast to predict whether a particular day is going to be an exceptional day to hunt, long before it takes place. As I discussed in Chapter 1, my passion for calculating high value days originated from a desire to make sure that when I did pull myself away from my family, friends or career, that I did so with an expectation of high potential. With limited resources of time and money, I have honed my interpretations of weather observations to the opportunities that I practice and discuss today. While I have studied other hunt predictors, none of them explain the massive amount of weather prediction experience gained not only from myself, but from those of my friends, readers, viewers and 100s of clients across the Country. To say that I keep circling back to the weather for my love of all things whitetail, including my career and passion for hunting, would be an understatement. A critical aspect that has been strengthened along my weather forecasting journey, is that the longer I have studied the weather, the greater the distance into the future I have experienced that you can predict a hunting value for a particular day.

Long Range Deer Forecasting

Decades ago, the best weather forecast source that I could find was the marine weather forecast that related to the Saginaw Bay area in Lake Huron, adjacent to the thumb region of Southeast MI. Several times in the mid 90s I left my home in Unionville or Caro to travel to my hunting land near Cass City, only to find that the wind direction forecast wasn't a fit for that morning's hunt based on the marine weather forecast. I would then do what any aspiring mature buck hunter would do; I would turn around and drive back home. My, how things have changed! The online weather sources, charts and graphs from sites like Weather Underground and AccuWeather, offer detailed looks into, not only the weather day yet to come, but for specific days, weeks or months from past decades. Your ability to see a week or more into the future and to plan for a major cold front within a day or two of it taking place, has of course never been better. In fact, if you haven't heard about an approaching cold front until it is only 4-5 days out, you really could not have been paying attention to the forecast. In the late 80s and early 90s, a day in advance was about all that we had within a level of reliable convenience. I licked my finger and stuck it up in the wind as much as anything. In the 2000s, 4-5 days out was acceptable; but now, in 2018, you should be able to recognize and plan for an approaching deerfront for more than a week before it happens.

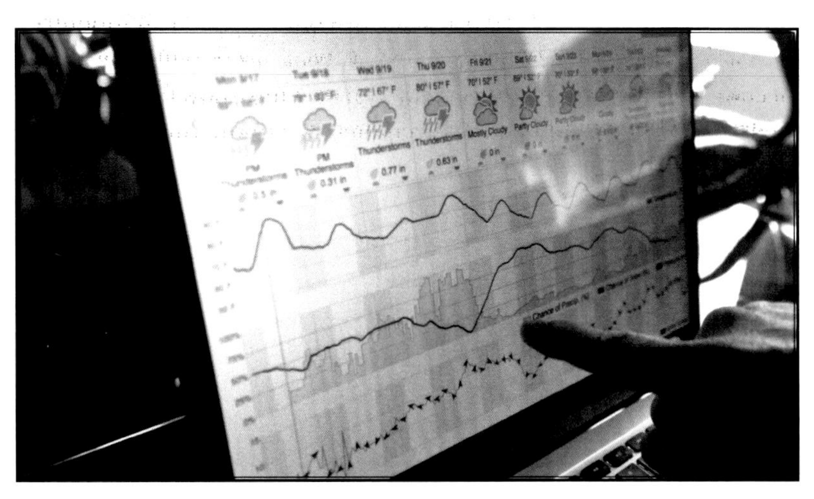

Tracking a major deerfront has never been easier with a variety of sources like Weather Underground and AccuWeather at your fingertips. The majority of extreme weather events can be discovered within the weather forecast up to 10 to 14 days out.

Tracking Major Deerfronts

You think you can't determine when a major deerfront is coming for more than a few days out? – Think again! A deerfront is any major change in the hunting season forecast, whether it is a warm front or a cold front. Both front types will significantly affect the calculations of deer hunting potential, for better or worse.

The beauty of a deerfront is that the majority of them begin to show themselves in the forecast a minimum of 10 days out. There should never be any surprises. Major fronts are created by the big picture of weather movements across North America, and not just by the local influences within the city, state or region that you live in. While you may not know the particular day it will hit, the exact temperature change, the specific wind speed, or even if there will be precipitation or not, you can easily see that something significant is going to take place. The accuracy rate of an approaching deerfront may be a lot more reliable than you may imagine.

Accurate Deerfront Expectations

While the exact time, temperature, wind speed or precipitation is an ever-approaching gray area, the fact that something is coming, rarely is. Within 24 hours of an expected deerfront taking place, I have experienced that 10-14 days out will deliver a "happening or not" accuracy rate of over 50%. A week away will deliver an accuracy rate of 80% or more, and within a few days the expected deerfront event will deliver an accuracy rate to the tune of 99%. I say 99% because is anything ever 100% certain in life?

That's more than a week away that you can talk to your spouse, your boss or your hunting buddy about. That's a week away that you can begin to plan for your sits and to make sure that you don't sit in your best stand just a few days before a much, much higher value sit opportunity will be taking place. Most of all, you have plenty of time to prepare in all ways for your next opportunity for a potential buck of a lifetime. There will always be a little gray area in the forecast, but not in the ways that it matters most.

Changing Deerfront Forecasts?

Temperature rules the roost when it comes to assessing the value of an upcoming day or two to hunt. While a 12-degree temperature drop may turn into 6 or 18 degrees, it's coming! Wind speeds are important but may vary greatly; however, wind direction is very important too, for deciding which treestand you ultimately choose to sit in. The great thing about wind direction forecasts, is that they are much more accurate than wind speed or precipitation levels. In fact, precipitation levels are often the least accurate ingredient of the weather forecast. But that's OK because precipitation levels are one of the least important aspects of determining the value of an upcoming sit. Probably the best aspect of an approaching deer cold front, is that a decrease in temperature can be picked out of the forecast at least 10-14 days out. Once you see a temperature drop still holding in the forecast at the 7-day mark and counting down, you know that you have a high quality event that you can alert all the need-to-knows in your life about, so that you can begin planning your next sit of a lifetime!

Conclusion

The beauty of the weather deerfront forecasting, is that the sources for professional weather forecasts only keep getting better. I actually believe that's why forecasting for deer has become so prominent in the world of whitetails as of late, because the huge advancements over single-day marine weather forecasts, are so significant. It is many times easier to recognize the trends and patterns in the weather that determine the potential for deer movement, as well as how the weather determines deer harvests, from decades ago. Did you shoot a giant buck on November 3rd of 1997, or during some other random date of decades past? With the information that will be revealed to you in the next chapter, you can determine the value of that hunting day, as well as the value of every other day that you killed a whitetail in the past, and every day that you will kill a deer, in the future.

Chapter 9

Priority of Whitetail Weather Influencers

Weather Factors

Listed are the ingredients that I believe have the greatest potential to bring havoc to the lives of whitetails. There are so many elements of deer-stressors that a whitetail has the potential of facing every day. Deer population dynamics, human pressure, habitat change, predators, breeding instincts, and fawning territory are just a few. However, arguably, none of those daily deer influencers carry more power than the urges of a whitetail's stomach.

A deer's rhythmic pattern of daily feeding activity is likely the most determining factor of deer movement during a 24-hour cycle, every day of the hunting season. Deer feed 5 times per day, and like a screaming baby, it's not hard to imagine that they don't like to miss their scheduled feedings. There are several slow moving, major changes, such as agricultural production or seasonal habitat shifts, that lead to a slow rise and decline of feeding conditions over several months. On a day to day basis, though, I have found no other collection of factors that so greatly influences a deer's stomach and his 24-hour movements that go along with their feeding urges, than the weather. In fact there is an entire list of weather features that individually carry their own level of power when it comes to dictating the hourly hunger pains of whitetails; in particular, when it comes to creating daylight movement!

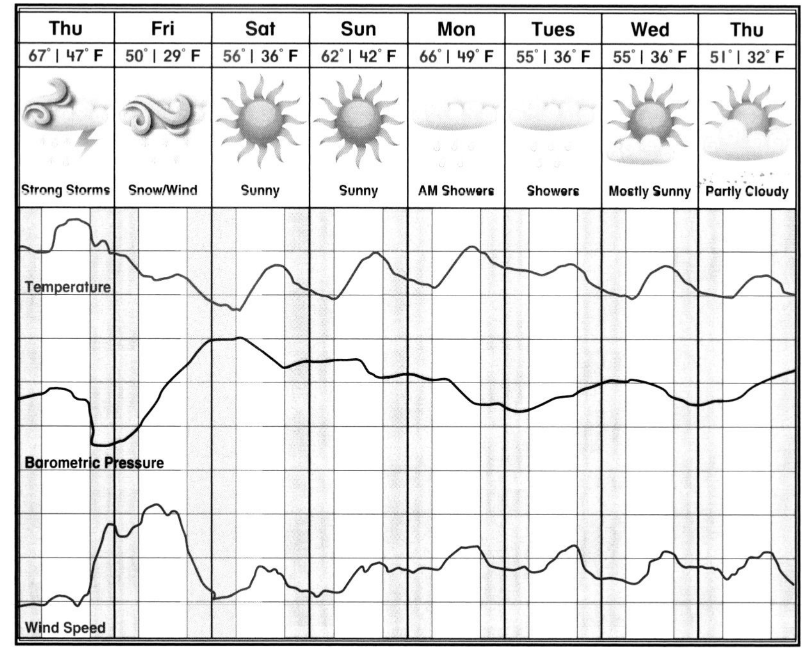

When extreme weather patterns clear, temperatures drastically drop and wind speeds diminish, it doesn't matter what time of the season it is, it's time to head to your favorite treestand.

Priority of Whitetail Weather Influencers

As you can imagine, after decades of experience using the weather to balance my hunting decisions, I have some very strong opinions for ranking the various weather ingredients. While they have all assisted me in building herds and hunting mature bucks to varying degrees, there are glaring weather condition differences in potential hunting value that rise far above the rest. Based on many years of success and failure along the way, here is my priority list for the greatest influencers of mature buck movement, in order of first to last:

Temperature – While nothing shuts down deer movement like a major blizzard, gale force winds or a thunderstorm, the change in temperature is what serves as the forecast's most positive instrument for determining the quality level of potential buck movement. High temperatures during the peak of the rut can be the kiss of death for daytime mature buck cruising opportunities; but on the flip-side, a significant decrease in temperatures of at least 8-10 degrees before, during, and most importantly, after the front, can create the conditions for memories to last a life time.

Winds – The best cold fronts carry the greatest wind speeds. It is not uncommon to have an October, November or December deer-hunting storm that carries 30-degree temperature drops, combined with over 40mph wind speeds, occurring at the same time. Like temperature change, wind speed change is all relative. I have experienced that a 20mph hour wind speed change from 45 to 25mph, isn't that much different in potential deer value than a decrease from 30 to 10mph. Hunting the lee side of cover and topographical changes are great tactics to practice during high winds, where deer are often sandwiched into a smaller area of protected portions of the habitat. However, when speeds take a dive, make sure that you are already in your favorite stand location, potentially entering during the cover of a wind storm.

The Setup – For a quality deerfront to take place, there needs to be a level of noticeable consistency. Periods of calm - boring and similar weather conditions that extend for several days - serve to set up and differentiate the drastic changes of a major weather event. When temperatures peak with clear skies and boring southerly winds for 5 days in a row, with 57, 61, 59, 58 and 57 degree temperatures, you can expect major deer movements to take place after extreme weather, major wind changes, and a significant temperature drop takes place.

Extreme Weather Conditions – Blizzards, thunder, heavy rain and high winds -the more extreme the better- all serve alone or in combination, to add fuel to the fire of a high-powered cold front. Major breaks within the extreme weather, and right before the weather change takes place, are good options, but the most reliable time to hunt is right after the conditions clear.

Barometric Pressure – The barometric pressure (bp), in my experience, is a highly misleading weather factor. For example, if major temperature changes take place, extreme weather subsides, there is a drastic change in wind speed, and the barometric pressure is low, the conditions to hunt still carry an extremely high value. Also, if those same conditions are present along with a rising barometric pressure, there is still a very high hunting value. If the temperatures are steady and rising with a random, high bp day mixed in due to a decrease in cloud cover, it is likely a poor day to hunt. The assumption is often that a high bp is a good day to hunt, when it is actually the change in the priority weather factors of temperature, wind, setup days and extreme weather, that creates a high value hunting opportunity – high barometric pressure or not. Is a high bp day a great day to hunt? Sure! If temps have fallen, wind speed has changed, and extreme weather is out of the picture. Often some of the best days to hunt combine an extreme drop in temperature and a rise in the barometric pressure. When that happens – hunt! However, that is only a small and basic portion of forecasting your own, high value hunting days. If weather influencers 1 through 4 are taking place, make sure not to miss out!

Moon – While the moon is not an actual weather influencer and could technically be ranked ahead of the bp, the bp is at least a reflection at times, of good things happening. However, the moon is not. Unless the weather factors of temperature drop, wind change, setup days and extreme weather have properly aligned first, the value of a particular high value day can't be assigned. Something I like to point out often is that a great moon forecast day with poor weather factors thrown in, is a poor day to hunt. However, a poor moon forecast day combined with great weather factors, is still a great day to hunt! The one moon factor I follow is when it is full and rising. I find that an evening sit value can be slightly diminished during a full moon, while the late morning feeding time can be enhanced. When the moon is full, deer can feed safely and socially all night long. I have experienced that deer are often bedded down at daybreak after an overly active nighttime, and feed less during their early morning daily time slot. This places a higher feeding priority for a late morning feeding binge, particularly when adjacent to bedding areas on high quality natural food sources, such as a remote cluster of apple trees or white oaks.

While the barometric pressure and various moon phases may slightly influence feeding times, neither can come close to comparing to the extreme weather patterns of temperature, wind, rain, snow and thunder.

The Ability To Influence Feeding Times

Imagine a giant buck hidden and bedded on a wooded point deep in the forest. His bedding area is located within an outcropping of rocks, several scattered red cedars and briar patches, with the occasional canopy of a few giant mature oaks. It is the middle of the day and he has one thing on his mind - Food! His hunger urges will lead him towards his favorite afternoon food source. However, there is a weather factor that will slow him down or speed him up. What truly has the ability to influence his feeding time the most?

I ask that you use a heavy dose of common sense when it comes to deciding what truly has the power to impact a deer's hunger pains. The moon or the barometric pressure – really? How about a major blizzard or extreme winds! When it comes to creating the need to feed or the desire to shelter in place, it doesn't take a whole lot of imagination to relate a deer's tendencies to the priority of potential weather factors. There are obvious influencers of deer movement that carry a huge amount of power on their own, and there are other factors that are obviously not that much of an influence by themselves.

Conclusion

If you were alone, lost and afraid in some Northern wilderness location, what would carry the greatest weight to negatively impact your predicament? The barometric pressure? The Moon? Or how about an extreme weather event of snow, rain, sleet, temperature change or winds. The weather ingredients that have the most potential to deliver an enormous level of havoc in the deer woods, are not that different from what would carry the highest potential of disaster if we as hunters were lost in the wilderness somewhere. Just like whitetails experience after a major weather event passes through, when we are finally rescued from being lost, cold, stressed, and starved, we would eat – and eat heavily! A whitetail's stomach often rules the day, all year long. The various weather features have the ability to create hunger pains like no other natural occurrence in a deer's daily battle with mother nature, humans and predators. By molding your hunting opportunities around the weather induced feeding urges of a mature buck that you are after, you can find a highly defined hunt that offers you the greatest chance when he is on his feet during the hours of daylight.

Chapter 10

Priority of Whitetail Weather Influencers

Hours before his evening feeding, the giant buck began to feel the subtle hints of change in the air. The Easterly winds turned from the North and finally from the Northwest, with an increasing bitterness of a significant early November cold front. With each explosive gust, the stress of creaking trunks and breaking branches grew, as the full force of the storm had yet to reach it's climax. The unseasonably warm daytime high of 67 continued to plummet, and the old recluse began to feel the pains of hunger created through energy losses that were being attacked by both cold and stress. The diminished glow of the rising moon did little to relax the buck as the full force of the storm kept him pinned down within his daytime hideaway. He cautiously stood and moved a few yards to browse on a squirrel's stash of several acorns, as well as the tender buds of young aspen shoots. The crack of a nearby mature oak increased his heart rate to a level equal to the time when a pack of coyotes were howling nearby. After standing motionless for nearly an hour, the buck returned to his nearby bed, effectively squashing any lingering thoughts of heading to his favorite afternoon food source, let alone following through with any of his rutting instincts. After a cold, dark, and significantly stress-filled night, the buck began to sense that calming conditions were on the horizon. After missing 5 feeding opportunities, a 20-degree temperature drop, and over 24 hours had passed, the great beast pulled his energy depleted magnificent frame to a standing position, and the primal urges of both feeding and rutting desires took over. He was ready – ready to move early, ready to move with a predictable purpose, and ready to expose himself to a hunter who had recognized an incredible weather enhanced rut hunting opportunity.

November 3, 2008 - During a toe-numbing morning sit, this monster fought a serious daybreak battle over a doe in estrus, while he made dozens of rubs at the same time. Later in the day he was still with her when I shot him, ending an exhausting 4 day rut hunt with extremely cold early November temperatures.

The Foundation of Food

Although research confirms that the whitetail rut takes place at virtually the exact same time in your area every hunting season, most hunters know that all ruts are not created equal. As much as a hunter's head can spin with the mental images of scrapes, full moons, rubs, monster bucks, and the magic of a major chase scene, the best day to be in a rut-crazed woods will rarely be a set date on a calendar that can be predicted months in advance.

My system is simple, and its foundation begins with food. A deer's stomach dictates so much of it's daily movement pattern. Food should not only be the foundation for your hunting strategy during the entire season, but for the entire rut. Deer are rhythmic pattern feeders and typically feed 5 times during a 24-hour period. I believe you can relate. When you miss a meal, you become hungry!

In 2014 I developed a formula to express a value rating for using the forecast fluctuations of temperature, weather extremes, heat and wind to define exactly when to recognize an upcoming high-quality sit during the entire hunting season. This formula was later published in the 2015 November rut issue of October Life, as their feature article. I did my best to reflect the weather factors that I have used for decades to predict exactly when to head to a stand. This formula has worked for October Lull sits, during all phases of the rut, during the early or late archery seasons, and believe it or not, during all 365 days of the year, whether you are hunting, scouting or just plain love to observe deer. Regardless of when the annual explosion of rutting activity takes place in your area, or when you are actually considering your next deer hunt within or outside of the annual whitetail rut, you can rely on a variety of weather factors to reveal some of the best sit opportunities during the entire hunting season.

November 6, 2004 - After watching this 10 point buck in 2003, lose the battle for a doe to the buck that I later killed that same day, he blew up into a heavy 13 point, for a picture perfect high value blue sky hunt.

Create Your Own Whitetail Forecast

Some of the best whitetail weather high value days to sit in a tree each season, include toe numbing mornings, clear blue skies, and at times even a little snow. However, let the whitetail weather prediction followers beware because not all forecasts will lead you to a level of precision success. The formula that will be revealed to you shortly, relies on decades of proven tactics which you can apply to, not only hunting this season, but for choosing days to hunt during every hunting season for the rest of your life! Also, make sure to read to the entire end of this chapter to discover the easiest and most basic deer forecasting tip of them all for making sure that you don't miss the best days to be in the woods with a single glance at the forecast.

Following various deer forecast calendars and your favorite day of the month of October or November to hunt, can be hit or miss at best. Even the most popular deer forecasts rely on a heavy dose of coincidence to hit the actual best days to be in the woods. Meaning, most deer forecasts guess, at best. Why? Because if the priority of weather factors don't hit just right, then any forecast that prioritizes barometric pressure, the moon or some magic date of the hunting season, in my experience, will lead you astray.

October 22, 2011 - During the beginning of the Pre Rut I found myself in the wrong location during a cold evening sit, while two distant giants fought across the field for a hot doe. Suddenly this illusive target buck came sneaking my way towards one of our water holes.

While no prediction is perfect, including mine, you can still significantly narrow your whitetail forecast efforts while playing a highly consistent hand of poker, every time that you climb into your favorite treestand. The weather can be used to forecast the potential of your success, for good or bad. The key factors to follow are these:

1. **Temperature**
2. **Wind**
3. **Extreme Weather**
4. **Stability**
5. **Moon (last and least)**

By learning how to use all 5 of the deer feeding weather priority factors to forecast which day to be in the woods, you will be well on your way to pulling the trigger on your best target buck every deer season. The most consistent high value days to climb into a tree, rely on the most predictably unstable weather patterns. If you are a numbers kind of a person, I will provide plenty of math for your enjoyment; however, if you prefer results, make sure to check out some of the examples below of how these 5 factors were specifically used to create proven results.

November 5, 2013 - During the Summer months we greatly enjoyed watching this beautiful droptine buck feed lazily in the neighbors fields nearly a mile away. An early November cold front sent him cruising my way while I was perched on a freshly hung treestand in a narrow pinch-point between two wood lots.

Barometric Pressure Factors

The barometric pressure (bp) is like the moon – something that you just can't put your finger on. In fact, you can't really feel it at all. At least you can see the moon. One could assume that deer can somehow feel the bp changes – whether the bp is actually rising or falling. However, I have experienced that deer do not react to some unseen or unfelt factor like the bp. Instead, deer react to changing wind directions, rises and fall of wind speed and clearing extreme weather patterns. The bp should be considered a non-factor because it is really not a physical factor that has the power to influence deer movement in any way. The bp is a reflection of physical weather changes; but the physical portions of the weather, and to a much lesser extent the moon, carry the true power to influence deer movements. Just like various moon phases can be extremely misleading hunt predictors unless the true priority weather ingredients are taking place first, the bp can be highly misleading, whether it is relied upon for a priority or minority of potential influence. Winds, rain, snow, heat, cold, thunder and lightning – each of these weather priorities – carry the potential to cause havoc in the deer woods, and deer can actually see, hear and feel their effects. The bp and moon cannot create havoc in the deer woods - in any way! Instead, deer react to the rise and fall of bp based on the weather factors that influence the change, first and foremost. The potential intensity for influence is the foundation for my whitetail weather forecast prediction formula.

October 29, 2014 - The first high value morning sit on a new property in a new stand location delivered both a nice buck and a doe with a very high level of predictability.

Whitetail Weather Prediction Formula

Unfortunately, math is boring. The good thing about math though, is that calculations can be used to accurately assign levels of predictability in many areas, including when it comes to forecasting your next whitetail hunt of a lifetime! If you don't care for the shear boredom of numbers, make sure to skip ahead. However, if you want to engage in a mathematical formula that can deliver during the rut or any other portion of the hunting season, here you go:

1. **Calm Days before the front/Poor Value Days:** 2days=1 point, 3days=3 pts, 4days=8 pts, 5days=10 pts

2. **Temp Change (pre-post front):** +2 Points for every temp drop up to 20 degrees(2-40pts)

3. **Top Wind Speed During Front:** 1-10=1point,11-15=5pts, 16-20=7pts,20+=10pts(1-10 pts)

4. **Extreme Conditions During Front:** +2 each for extreme rain, wind (25+mph), snow, sleet, and thunder (0-10 pts)

5. **Wind Speed Post Front:** 0-10mph=5 pts, 11-15=3 pts, 16-20=1 point (1-5 pts)

6. **Value For Each Day After Front:** Day 1=Full Value, Day 2 x.67, Day 3 x.33

7. **Moon Phase:** +5 for Full Moon late morning sits, -5 for Full Moon Evening sits, +5 for dark moon evening sits (+/-5 pts)

I do not expect most folks to fully calculate every day that they want to hunt during the whitetail rut, the early season, the late season or even during Summer scouting missions. However, I developed this formula to accurately reflect the conditions that, not only do I personally use to determine my own deer hunting forecasts each season, but this formula accurately reflects the majority of my buck harvests dating back nearly 25 years! If you learn the concepts of this formula, you will be headed towards a highly predictable level of success every Fall, along with 365 days out of the year!

November 29, 2015 - A two day temperature drop and a cool evening sit, delivered this long range cruising monster buck within bow range, on the last day of Wisconsin's annual riffle season.

Weather Forecasting Basics

The best days to hunt during each season rely heavily on 3 critical factors: Temperature drops of 8-10 degrees or more, wind speed changes of 8-10mph or more, and the various weather priority conditions have ceased - rain, snow, thunder and lightening. When those conditions take place after a major deerfront has passed, make sure not to miss the first calm, cold, evening and morning sit. That's it folks! If you can also get 3-5 days of calm, warm and consistent days to take place before the front passes, then your sit opportunity gets even better!

If you keep an eye on the forecast for the buck movement triggers of temperature, wind and pressure, you can create your own forecast for just about any day of the entire year - whether you are scouting from February to September, or hunting during any portion of the hunting season.

October 31, 2016 - Dylan Lenz called this nice five year old buck Diego and the name stuck. A huge cold front that passed early on October 30th sent Diego right past my treestand the next morning before my toes even had a chance to freeze during the early morning below average temperatures.

10 out of 10 Precision Formula Forecasts

The best way to discuss the process of using my weather formula to predict the highest value days to be in the woods, is by example. While there are examples of successful buck hunts woven throughout this chapter, there are two special hunts that I wanted to highlight and calculate the hunting value for.

The conditions for my 2007, 15 point buck, were forecasted a week in advance. Major cold fronts are hard to miss when they pop up in the weather report, and the 2007 late October front was no exception! Even the moon, which has been proven to not play any role in the actual timing of the rut, contributed a small influence for the potential movement of this buck. The details of the forecast led to a perfect score of 10 out of 10, when using my rut prediction:

October 26th, 2007 15 Point, Morning Sit

1. **Moon:** +5 (Full moon rising during evening)
2. **Temp Change:** +40 (5-day drop)
3. **Wind Speed Post Front:** +5 (5mph)
4. **Top Wind Speed During Front:** +10 (Greater than 20mph)
5. **Extreme Conditions:** +2 (43mph winds)
6. **Calm Days:** +8 (4 days slow drop)

   Calculation: 70 points/7=10 Value Sit

After 4 straight days (+8 points) of both calm and poor hunting conditions to enhance the effects of the 20 degree temperature drop (+40 points), the foundation was created for a high value Pre Rut morning sit. With a full moon rising (+5 points) during the evening hours, the deer experienced a roller coaster of high level feeding and social activities that created a peak forecast for potential movement following a major weather front that included top wind speeds of over 43 mph (10 points for over 20 mph +2 for extreme wind conditions). The cool and calm 5mph wind forecast (+5 points) for the morning of the sit was the final ingredient to make sure that this morning was a sure-fire "10" based on the high value hunt prediction algorithm. After adding together the hunt prediction points described in the paragraph, they equal 70 (8+40+5+10+2+5). When divided by 7 the total value is a "10".

A High Value Peak Rut Prediction Example

When warm weather takes a bite out of the middle of a week-long rut hunt, what do I suggest that you do? Don't hunt! By saving my best cruising rut stand locations for a high value day, I was rewarded with a 173" gross target buck monster the first time using the stand location. Every year the majority of high value sits are squashed days or weeks ahead of time, by impatient hunters. How do you kill more bucks by sitting on the couch? By letting your best stands improve when they remain completely unpressured. Make sure to not turn a perfect "10" into a dud "1" by using the stand during warm weather and high winds, no matter what the moon phase or date on the calendar.

November 8th, 2005 "Turn Tine" Buck, Morning Sit

1. **Moon:** No moon impact
2. **Temp Change:** +28 (14 degree morning temp drop)
3. **Wind Speed Post Front:** +5 (8mph)
4. **Top Wind Speed During Front:** +10 (47mph gusts)
5. **Extreme Conditions:** +2 (47mph winds)
6. **Calm Days:** +10 (5 day slow warm up)

   Calculation: 55 points/7=7.8 Value Sit

While a 7.8 value day may not seem very high compared to a perfect "10", it was certainly more than passing! Very few days during the hunting season calculate to a score of 7 or over. Many are below 3, and there are a few between 4 and 7, but what I have experienced is that less than 25% of all hunting days can capture a score of 7 or higher. When a 7 or higher pops up in the forecast – make sure to take notice! In fact, Thursday, November 10th, was the first day in La Crosse, WI that scored over a 4 since October 30th. With several warm days preceding the 10th, I left on Monday to return home for work and family, waiting for the Thursday prediction of a high value day. The significant improvement in value led to a first sit reward, for an incredible target buck!

November 3, 2018 - Two days of falling temperatures, a break in the rain and quiet Southeast early morning winds, set the stage for a rewarding hunt in a brand new stand location. The stand location scouted ten months earlier for those exact same conditions and patience paid off.

Conclusion

As I think back to the majority of my top 25 buck kills, nearly all of them fell within the 8-10 value of whitetail weather formula calculations. However, many hunters do not have the time or passion to actually sit down and figure out the values for each and every day of the hunting season. The good news? You don't have to! Instead, by keying on major temp drops, wind speed changes and rising pressure sits, you will notice a significant trend of incredible deer activity. While the bp is not a priority weather factor, it can be used to reflect outstanding conditions in one very basic, quick observation: When temperatures decrease to their lowest point in the forecast, and the barometric pressure increases to its highest point in the forecast, make sure to head to the woods! There is also one more factor to add to the equation that may make the season even more successful: If the morning temps are below 32 and you know for certain that your toes are going to get a little numb, make sure not to miss out! Freezing temperatures have a history of pushing mature bucks to their feet, even if the daytime high predictions are in the 50s or higher. Whether you are focusing on freezing morning temperatures, or weather forecast days that feature a score of 7 or higher, you can use my whitetail formula to guide you to success every day of the season, all season long.

Chapter 11

The Build-Up to the Annual Whitetail Rut

The time frame was on or just after, October 1st, in the late 80s. I was a teenager and with a 5-acre woodlot full of rubs and surrounded by corn, I just couldn't resist sneaking into a pre-hung stand. An early September stealthy scouting mission revealed a bachelor group of bucks lazily bedding the hot hours of the sun away within the woodlot, before taking a late afternoon stroll to a hay field across the corn to the South. With the morning temperatures hovering around freezing for an early bow season hunt, the perfect deerfront had passed to create an incredibly high value, daybreak sit opportunity. Well at least as an inexperienced teenage hunter, that's what I thought.

Calculating both high and low value sit opportunities has been the foundation of my hunting success on both public and private lands, since the early 90s. Each season new weather forecasting details are learned and reinforced to effectively and efficiently play poker in the deer woods. However, a high value day, does not necessarily mean that you should sit in a deer stand all day. There are values within the daily values, and to simplify the process of understanding deerfronts and how they should be hunted, has as much to do with the time of day within the time of the season, as it does the actual value of the day itself.

While deer go through obvious annual biological phases of birth to feeding to breeding to survival, all year long, I have experienced that they are ushered quickly through a compact combined set of 12 hunting and biological steps, throughout the hunting season. The first 4 steps of the season begin the climb to the explosion of deer activity during the annual whitetail rut and include the bow season opener, the early bow season, the October lull and the

Pre Rut. Each day during each of the 12 steps of deer activity, carries a potential value based on the weather, and once a high value day is discovered within the forecast, you can learn to prioritize the portion of the day that you should focus on most.

The Bow Season Opener

"Mid value mornings, High value evenings"

No one in our family hunted, so it was easiest for my brother and me to request Darton 30MX bows for Christmas, and then be dropped off as a couple of teenagers on private land to figure out deer hunting on our own. I can still remember how exciting it was for our first, opening day! We didn't care if it was morning, evening, or mid-day; we just wanted to go deer hunting. We spooked deer, missed deer, and due to the lack of any treestands, I am sure that we came close to falling out of trees while standing on branches, more than once. Many years later the practice of bowhunting for myself has become a lot more disciplined, and therefore, a whole lot more successful. "Discipline" is a key word, when the bow season opener rolls around each season.

The lazy last days of Summer, fat and lazy deer herds and woodlots that haven't been bombarded by the onslaught of rut hunters and gun hunters, allow bowhunters to calmly step into an unsuspecting herd and take their chances. This opportunity begs a question - should the opening day of bow season that is marked on your wall calendar, be your opening day on your treestand in the woods? I believe a level of great whitetail reward can be found by exercising a good dose of patience. In every phase of the hunting season moving forward, I like to first identify a great day to sit, and then to identify the best time(s) of the day to sit.

Bow season opening mornings have undoubtedly accounted for 10s of thousands of mature bucks throughout the decades of modern-day hunting pursuits. However, those same opening day mornings have accounted for even more spooked deer that lead to spooked deer herds, that have eventually lead to entire spooked hunting lands. While I love to sneak into a remote, downwind bedding area or lengthy travel corridor morning stand location, I only do so when I believe that a mature buck is definitely using that particular bedding area. I only risk a morning hunt if I can wrap around the outside and away from morning feeding locations, during a high value day. Finally, I will only consider hunting an opening morning stand location if it isn't in the same afternoon feeding movement of a higher potential evening stand location opportunity. I think that an opening morning of bow season hunt has been proven over and over again, to carry a potential level of success; however, make sure to place a premium on evening sits at this time of the year, by not spooking the deer in the morning in their lazy late Summer line of daily deer movement.

Although an early season morning hunt is not out of the question, make sure not to sit in a morning treestand location that has the potential of diminishing the value of a more premium evening sit opportunity.

Early Bow Season

"Low value mornings, High value evenings"

The difference between an opening day of bow season sit, and an early bow season sit is that, "The gig is up", as they say. Hunters have already entered the woods, and although I have experienced many times over that one 40-acre parcel can be viewed as a much lower risk factor in the local deer herd's heads, the potential of deer feeding lazily in open fields in the morning, has been greatly reduced, even if that potential has been affected by the neighbor's hunting activities across the fence line, and not your own. Although you may have a long transition of open hardwoods to cover from the perfectly placed treestand, there is a high likelihood that a particular buck you are after is already in his bed. Also, a good morning transition stand is often an outstanding evening stand location, by allowing you to place yourself near a buck's bedding area for his late afternoon, bedding area exit. During the early bow season, unless the conditions of morning movements - long transitions areas and the perfect non-invasive access routes - are present, it pays to capture the highest value the day has to offer, which is typically during an evening hunt.

The October Lull

"Mid value mornings, High value evenings"

The October Lull begins when the cumulative amount of hunting pressure applied to hunting lands, effectively moves the local deer herd to safer habitats. I have experienced that the October Lull is a myth. Deer still move and feed 5 times in a 24-hour period, but they often just do it in another portion of the neighborhood that has experienced significantly reduced levels of hunting pressure. This is also when the effects of the annual whitetail shift, are taking place.

The "annual whitetail shift" is a phrase that I coined years ago, to describe the annual migration of bucks, and sometimes doe family groups, as they move from their Summer habitats to their Fall habitats. While this annual phenomenon begins to take place in September when the beans turn brown, hunters first hit the woods, and the last cutting of hay is harvested, the shift gets slammed into overdrive, leaves begin to drop and opening day of bow season has already taken place. The shift of bucks is as much a shift of cover and food choices, as it is hunting pressure. Gone are Summer food and cover sources, which also leads bucks into their preferred, Fall and Winter, high stem count daytime bedding locations that could not have been used during the Summer period of velvet growth. If your Fall hunting grounds offer high quality food and cover options, as well as low or undetectable amounts of hunting pressure, you should actually see an influx of deer, in particular bucks, during the otherwise dreaded October Lull.

During the October Lull there is a great deal of opportunity for someone following cold weather deerfronts, especially on lands that possess quality Fall food and cover. Sporadic high value morning sits can be found when the skies are clear, cold and calm, in particular, the first morning frosts of the year. My best MI bow buck came during an October 12th morning following 50+mph winds and a star-lit, frosty night. Although evening sits are the high value of the day during this time of year, don't forget about high value morning opportunities.

When numerous major scrapes start popping up in the woods, not only is a mature buck likely around but the Pre Rut has begun. If you have mature bucks on your land, you will find that the beginning of Pre Rut buck sign takes place at the same time every year.

The Pre Rut

"High value mornings, mid value evenings"

The Pre Rut begins a period of change in deer behavior which is not induced by hunters. While the majority of the periods of time leading up to the rut are strongly influenced by hunting pressure, I find Pre Rut activities taking place like clockwork, every single season. In most Northern states that means the last 10 days of October something magical takes place IF, 2 very important ingredients are present, including: Cold overnight temperatures and mature bucks.

The occurrence of enjoying the excitement of the Pre Rut on your land, I have experienced to be directly parallel to the presence of mature bucks. No mature bucks, no Pre Rut. Have you ever wondered why on your land rubs, scrapes, grunts and mature buck sightings are popping up like someone just poured them out of a can; while your buddy across the state is seeing nothing at all? You can just about always blame that happening on the availability of older bucks, or not.

Each year that a buck grows, he lays down more and more sign. I value that assumption when I scout public land, when I look at new private parcels to hunt and when I choose to hunt a particular area of the parcel. If I see no evidence of an accumulation of old or new sign I either move on to a new parcel or in the case of this season's potential Pre Rut hunting opportunities - another stand location.

Although bucks may not be moving all day, they sure have a way of blowing up their lazy morning habits and replacing them with a supercharged fury of rutting movement. If the temperatures are unseasonably warm, just wait a few more days for the temperatures to dip and he action will significantly pick up. Although the doe herd isn't typically quite ready yet, the mature bucks know the game, and they are in the mood when the daytime values are high! A great indicator of the beginning of the Pre Rut is when waterhole use suddenly becomes very apparent during the morning hours. All night rutting activity attributes to sudden morning waterhole use, and I have personally witnessed this since the early 2000s.

While Pre Rut evening can be hot the last hour of the day, I have used the first 5 hours of toe-numbing, morning Pre Ruts in the past, to kill some of my oldest and biggest archery bucks.

Conclusion

As you can guess, my teenage opening day of bow season morning hunt back in the mid-80s, ended up being over before it started. After a ½ mile walk through the rows of corn, any deer that was going to or already inside the woodlot, had to be gone before I was within ¼ mile of reaching my treestand. For all of the scouting time and preparation, the hunt was actually not a waste. I had learned a hard lesson that going into a great stand at the wrong time of the day, during the wrong time of the season, could destroy the effectiveness of a great location for weeks to come. Hunting that woodlot at that time of the year, was a zero out of 10 no matter what the value of the forecast was.

Choosing the right high value day to hunt, and then choosing the perfect stand for the appropriate time of the day to hunt for the given time of the season, is a pattern that can help you choose the best stand location for whitetail success, for decades to come. Choosing a great stand during the build-up to the annual rut is important because opportunities are fewer and further between. However, when the true intensity of the whitetail rut begins during the middle portions of the season, choosing the best days to sit can reveal an explosion of buck intensity that can make your heart pound and your head spin – several times in the same day!

Chapter 12

The Extreme Roller coaster of Rut and Gun

During the hunting season there is no greater impact on deer than by hunters, which creates a roller coaster of low, mid and high value hunting opportunities within each time period of a particular day. When the hunting season moves forward into rut and featured gun seasons, a mixing bowl of hunter pressured rut crazed bucks reach a climax of incredible hunting opportunity!

The following is a step by step guide for making sure that you get the highest score for each and every high value day in the forecast, no matter where that day falls, within the middle of the 12 different phases of the hunting season. I would like you to think of each sit that you choose to take, as falling within a score of 1-10. After first predicting a high value day is available for that sit - sometimes even during the morning and the evening sit. In fact, as the rut continues, a case can be made for scoring not only the morning and evening hunt for a possible 20 out of 20 score for the entire day, but you can add a mid-day value sit for a potential score of 30 out of 30 for the entire day. While the Pre Rut finishes the climb to most extreme deer movements of the entire season, the Lock Down phase has an interesting way of noticeably slowing it down.

The Lock Down Phase

**"Mid value mornings, Mid value mid-days,
Mid value evenings"**

During the Pre Rut, the old boys know exactly what's about to happen, the does nervously await the changes coming soon, and I believe the young bucks aren't really sure what to think. The sudden, aggressive nature of a mature buck has got to rile up the entire herd, let alone the young bucks that finally realize they probably need to choose their sparring partners very wisely.

There are a small percentage of does entering estrus, and for a week to 10 days the rutting activity is in a holding pattern. But, then it happens!

The annual rut lock down phase begins when a high percentage of does begin to enter their estrus cycles. More and more does begin to come into estrus, to the point that nearly every buck gets invited to the initial breeding party. Individual bucks only breed a handful of does at best each season, and I believe that the first does that bucks breed during the rut, are pretty easy pickings. In fact, from what I experience on an annual basis, sometime during the first 4-5 days of November in SW WI, there is a noticeable shut down of rutting activity and overall deer movements for at least 3-4 days.

The annual rut lock down phase still features some great hunting opportunities, but you just never know when a particular buck that meets your standards, is going to finish with one doe after 2-3 days of chasing, tending, fighting and breeding, and then seek for another. Finding morning hunting locations that relate to buck and doe bedding, mid-day cruising hotspots that are surrounded by major bedding or food source locations, and then stand locations that relate to afternoon food source movements, can each help you navigate the highest values per day during the lock down phase. However, make sure that your stand locations make sense for the time of the day that you are hunting. For example, a food source movement hunt may carry the potential for a very high value in the evening, but a very poor value for a morning hunt. Likewise, an exceptional morning stand that relates to remote bedding areas, may be a very poor choice the closer it gets to dark, because nearly every deer in the woods has already left their bedding areas and are heading towards their favorite afternoon food sources.

While the Peak Rut can carry crazy buck movements across your entire hunting land at any moment of the day, a lock down strategy that uses highly defined stand locations to capture the best potential movement for a given portion of the day, is a wise choice. During the lock down phase, finding more than 1 stand location to use during the same day of hunting, is highly appropriate.

Maximizing the value of an all day Peak Rut sit most often means that you need to use at least two treestand locations: one morning stand that relates to bedding areas and another stand that relates to afternoon food source movements.

The Peak Rut

"High value mornings, High value mid-days, Mid value evenings"

If you have a specific target buck that you are after, the weeks leading up to the Peak Rut features the perfect time to set your sites on a buck that is in a defined pattern on the lands that you hunt. If you have a giant running around near daylight, before the Peak Rut, don't wait! Once you reach the Peak Rut, all bets are off! While the time to shoot a target buck is before the Peak Rut begins, the time to shoot any buck in the neighborhood is during the Peak Rut, at any time of the day.

The beauty of the Peak Rut is that opportunity can present itself at any moment. However, don't be fooled into the belief that every great treestand location can command the attention of the local buck herd all day long. In fact, I have experienced that you need to make sure that you are using stand locations that offer you a great chance at a buck during all 3 phases of daylight, including morning, mid-day and evening. As in the lock down phase, stand locations that focus on bedding areas in the morning, food and bedding during the mid-day, and then food sources in the afternoon, should be considered, even if that means using 2 to 3 stand locations during the same day.

The Post Rut

"High value mornings, Mid value mid-days, High value evenings"

Unlike during the Pre Rut period of the hunting season when mature bucks are overly anxious to kick off the annual rut, during the Post Rut those same bucks just can't seem to let go. While the bulk of the does have already been bred during the primary rut, I have experienced that bucks still hold onto their daily rut patterns of cruising, checking out doe family group feeding or bedding areas, and keeping their scraping habits alive. The Post Rut is an exceptional time to shoot a wandering monster buck from ½ mile away or more, as he continues to seek, attempt to find, and then to potentially breed his last doe of the primary rut. The Post Rut often finds bucks taking big chances to step into other mature buck's territories and to travel great distances during the primary rut's last flurry. Once a series of low value days climb into the forecast, I find that Post Rut activity takes a sharp decline to a near certain end, unless a mid-November cold front revives the movement for a few days longer.

During the Pre Rut I have experienced that, although a mature buck's daylight activity level is on the rise, his movements largely take place during the morning, and then partially during the afternoon. The Post Rut is similar, but I find that there is more value that can be experienced for observing the oldest bucks in the neighborhood, during the mid-day and afternoon hours, as well as still a high value during the morning hours. Some of my Peak Rut morning sits that have revealed sightings of 10-12 bucks of all ages by noon, turn into 6 older bucks, on average, from two stands at all times of the day during the Post Rut. During this time of the hunting season I encourage you to weigh your stand choices heavily towards bedding areas during the morning hours and adjacent to afternoon food sources during an afternoon sit. However, keep in mind that doe family groups have been pestered for 3 to 4 weeks at this point, and they may not be entirely receptive to an unwelcome guest!

During 2006 I had the pleasure of sitting on a treestand covering the corner of a 550-yard food plot, hidden by CRP growth within a remote corner of the land. It was mid-November, and the beginning of gun season was just a couple of days away. I was right in the middle of the Post Rut, and when a group of does and fawns exited their bedding areas during a high value deerfront day and scattered in front of me, I was extremely hopeful. And then he came! He was slow, deliberate, dark, heavy and methodical in his movements, heading straight towards the fawns that were clustered together within 25 yards of my stand. The fawns began to look at him as he slowly cleared the slight rise in front of me to expose himself, and he looked directly at them. My release was on my string and I just needed for him to turn to the right side to avoid allowing him to see me draw my bow. The fawns were extremely nervous at the sight of him. The does that were feeding 40-yards away snapped their heads towards him. The lead doe stomped her front toes at him, then blew, ran, and took all of the deer with her - including the buck! My heart sank, and a Post Rut opportunity that came so fast, exited just as quickly.

Tucking away, back in a remote corner of the woods near a mature buck bedding area, is a favorite tactic of mine, and I will often sit in that stand until early afternoon. However, when it comes to an evening hunt for a stressed-out doe herd, in hopes of finding a mature buck, I head straight for a hidden, doe-feeding hotspot for the last few hours of a Post Rut day.

One of my favorite opening day of gun season tactics is to place myself on the opposite side of heavy cover, from an overly aggressive neighbor.

Gun Season Opener

"High value mornings, High value mid-days, High value evenings"

The gun season opener is the one time that you can throw caution and high value calculations, to the wind. Even during the primary rut you can find poor value days combined with high value days based on the weather; however the value of an opening day sit is created by hunters, and I have experienced high quality opportunities on opening day, during all hours of the daylight. Which begs a question – why come out of the woods?

My favorite gun season tactic is to take a position on the opposite side of a large chunk of high quality cover from neighboring hunting pressure. While I expect this to be an outstanding stand location positioned within or on the edge of important mature buck daytime security cover, these stand locations can carry an extremely high value during the entire opening day. Best of all, if you access this stand location early, you can expect to be on the receiving end of hunter movements, from ½ mile to a mile in all directions. While there are times that I have enjoyed gun stands on the edge of fields or food plots during the evening hours, there is nothing better than climbing into a hidey hole alongside remote, mature buck bedding security cover. To spend an opening day observing what caliber of buck travels to his security cover in the morning, is spooked into it during the mid-day, or comes out of in the afternoon, is a great way to capture a high value gun season opener regardless of the weather, all day long.

Conclusion

The extreme roller coaster of the annual whitetail rut combined with majority of featured gun seasons across the Country, often seem to be over before they begin. Maybe you can relate; the older that I become, the shorter the frenzy of the rut and gun seasons seem to last. The middle portions of the season pass by quickly and take a lot of wind out of the sails of both man and beast. I believe that "Extreme" is one great way to describe the central portion of the annual hunt, and "Recovery" is an exceptional way to describe what follows.

Chapter 13

Late Season Deer Pressures

The recovery of the 3rd trimester of the annual whitetail season, is critical for both hunter and hunted. Pressured whitetails, worn out hunters and depleted habitats begin the swift decline towards a herd that is continuing to seek cover, food and security more every single day. A great late season All Weather Whitetail approach includes a heavy focus on recovering herds and a collection of afternoon treestand options.

Gun Season Post Opener

"Low value mornings, High value evenings"

The buck was traveling extremely slow from my right to my left, obviously cautious from 9 days straight of WI's 2015 gun season. The massive 6-year old stopped, methodically turned his head to look in all directions before proceeding, and then continued closer to my shooting window straight in front of me at 34 yards. There was still 25 more minutes of shooting light, but the dark clouds had shortened the window for a potential shot; and as he slowly closed the gap, my heart was racing incredibly hard! I fumbled but managed to connect my release to the string loop and was able to come to a complete draw before I stopped him in my shooting window with a nasally, "kneeee". The shot was clean and within seconds I had killed my 3rd largest buck with a bow, during the last few remaining minutes of the gun season.

While I prefer bowhunting, I don't mind gun hunting. I typically let the stand location and potential shooting lanes tell me what weapon to bring. In 2017 I hunted the entire opening day with a bow, and more than ½ of the entire gun season. The pattern of value that I have found, though, is if I am in thick cover, I use a bow, and if

I am in the open fields, I use a gun. However, there is nothing better than finding a high quality patch of daytime security cover to post up next to, to wait for a mature buck to exit out of just before dark.

Of course, you can kill a buck in the morning hours during the waning days of the annual gun season, but while opening day can bring huge opportunity cruising your way at daybreak, I have experienced that by the 2nd day, mature buck activity takes a severe dive until the afternoon hours. I urge you to place a huge premium on post opening day evening gun hunts, in particular when you can observe remote buck bedding exit routes, or a hidden food source next to high value security cover that has not been infringed upon by hunters. Secure cover is rare after the gun season opener, so don't be surprised if the oldest buck in the neighborhood realizes that fact, too.

By the time the late season rolls around in high pressure states like MN, WI, MI, PA, IN, OH and NY, if your deer blinds aren't hidden, every deer in the neighborhood likely knows where they are at. And that's not a good thing!

Secondary Rut

"Mid value mornings, mid value mid-days, High value evenings"

The secondary rut is what I believe to be a hidden gem of whitetail opportunity. Once you narrow down the timing of the lock down phase in your area, which is a period of time that a large number of does enter estrus, then you just need to add 28 days and make sure not to miss out! That places the lock down phase in my SW WI hunting grounds, during the first several days of December. In Southern OH that would equal the middle of December, and in Kansas that could equal the 3rd week of December. While there are a very limited number of days, they can be as powerful as the Peak Rut. Great opportunities can be found all day long, but the evening hours really stand out!

During the middle of November and later in most Northern states, temperatures are falling, forage supplies are shrinking, and whitetails are becoming much hungrier. This places a priority for hunting the afternoon hours, as deer are predictably traveling towards high quality food sources on a daily basis. No matter what period of the season from the bow season opener to the end of the late archery season, you should avoid spooking out a higher evening sit potential by risking a lower value morning sit. While there are some fairly good potential morning and mid-day opportunities during the secondary rut, don't forget about the high value of an evening sit when you are analyzing the deer forecast and planning your upcoming sits.

Late Season Muzzleloader

"Low value mornings, High value evenings"

In Chapter 6, I discussed the story of both one of my greatest hunting experiences, and at the same time, one of my greatest hunting blunders. The value that I experienced the afternoon of that fateful hunt, was absolutely incredible. A wicked snowstorm had whipped in several inches of snow, high winds, and a prolonged shut down of deer movements. However, when the storm wrapped up and cleared out, it combined for the perfect early December evening, muzzleloader hunt!

Just like you, I can't help myself and I venture out into a snow-filled morning muzzleloader hunt, especially when the temperatures are into the mid to high 30s or greater, and deer can be expected to be browsing adjacent to their bedding areas. However, extremely cold mornings that express temperatures well below freezing are great mornings to sleep in, enjoy being with the family and then use the afternoon hours to reap the rewards of hunting hungry whitetails that are figuratively putting the feed bag on! During December muzzleloader hunts, the value of a quality evening hunt during high value deer forecast days, is so high that you can make a case that they are the best days of the season to specifically target and kill the oldest buck in the entire neighborhood. I have clients who kill Boone and Crocket bucks during this period of the season nearly every single year. If you preserve the sanctuary of the land and afternoon food sources and allow those conditions to continue to repeat into December, you should not only not be surprised when a local legend steps into your crosshairs during an evening hunt, you should expect it.

Conifers, switchgrass, hardwood regeneration, briars, shrub tips and unpressured acres can attract the bulk of the neighborhood deer herd by the time late season archery comes into play. Focusing on afternoon food source movements is key to your success.

Late Season Bow

"Mid value mornings, High value evenings"

When the days on the calendar flip towards Christmas, into the New Year and beyond, deer have very few things on their mind, and you can easily use that to your advantage. The combination of food, survival and energy conservation, creates a ritualistic daily pattern of opportunity. You can expect whitetails feeding moderately on hidden pockets of woody browse during the morning to mid-day hours, and then heavy feeding during the afternoon if high quality food sources are still available. However, with a bow, your hunting strategy should turn into the cover towards afternoon travel corridors, located between bedding areas and the local whitetail herd's preferred afternoon food source.

In the early years, my hunting buddies and I used the end of archery to harvest as many does as we had tags for. The area in MI we hunted carried over 50 deer per square mile, and the stories seem endless about mishaps, frozen digits, backstraps and a whole lot of fun. In 10 years of hunting MI's Southern Thumb area, we saw 1 buck, after gun season – combined for all 10 years! However, the excitement we experienced by making sure, at all costs, not to spook deer in the morning so that we could find piles of whitetails to hunt during the evening hunt, was extremely rewarding. More than 2 decades later the value of an evening hunt during the late season has been firmly entrenched into my set of hunting strategies, regardless of whether I am targeting mature bucks or does.

Conclusion

From opening day of archery during the late Summer to the last and final day of archery season during the Winter I find it critical to make sure that I am attacking the particular period of the day that offers the highest potential value in the period of the hunting season that I am currently hunting. I want to stress to you that this does not mean that you can't shoot the oldest buck in the woods at a low value time of the day, on a low value day for that matter; however, a great deer hunting poker player is successful by consistently tilting the odds in his favor.

Multiple stands are most often needed to capture the highest daily values of whitetail potential, even during the peak of the rut. Is your favorite morning bedding area stand, the perfect fit for an evening sit? Probably not! Maximizing the value of every sit that you make during the morning, mid-day or evening hours, is no different than playing poker in the deer woods by choosing the best weather days to hunt. While the numbers of X out of 10 really does not mean much, trying to find the highest value in every sit truly does. The value of each sit that you choose to spend in the woods matters, but when you combine the potential of high quality hunting opportunities together with the value that hunting whitetails brings to the table to us all, we are truly blessed to be involved in such a high value passion. Whenever and wherever, we choose to sit!

Chapter 14

How to Stay Warm in the Deer Stand

The value of trying to stay warm when hunting deer is no joke, and if you hunt the best high value days of the season, the vast majority of them will be the coldest. Since the late 80s I have experienced that from -30 to +30 degrees, there are 4 critical parts to focus on to stay warm in your treestand: feet, core, hands and head. If you keep those 4 areas warm, you are well on your way to finding hot times in the frozen deer woods.

While keeping the feet, core, hands and head warm may seem like an obvious goal, what I have found since the mid 80s, is that it isn't as simple as it sounds. There are several tips I have learned throughout the decades for not only keeping the basics toasty warm, but doing so when you are sitting in a tree and hunting as a bowhunter, when excess noise and movement has to be factored in.

After being loaded down with enough gear to survive if a sub-zero afternoon sit, it is critical that you take all safety precautions when attempting to climb into your treestand.

High Value Deerfront Days

Just wear the most expensive clothes that money can buy, right? Well, I wish that was all that you had to do! While it doesn't make sense to skimp on hunting clothes that you expect to last for decades, there are several tips that I have found critical to my cold weather hunting success, in addition to, hunting in high quality clothes:

1. Keeping Your Feet Warm

Keeping my feet warm has been a career long roller coaster of literally, hot and cold results. I ask that you learn from over 30 years of toe numbing experiences so that you don't have to go through the same pain as I have! There are several "tried and true" toe warming methods that I have learned as the decades continue to roll by.

Dry socks can be a toe saver! By wearing lightweight socks on the way in, and then changing to both light and heavy layers when arriving at your stand or blind, your toes never need to experience the chill of damp socks!

When your socks are dry, adding a heat pack in the bottom of each boot can work extremely well. By carrying extra heat packs, you can wait until your feet are dry and cold a few hours after you climb into a stand or blind, and then add them when needed.

In a pinch, using an extra pair of insulated pants can help greatly by pulling them up to your knees, and then folding the remaining lower legs under your feet. This helps to not only insulate your feet, but to provide a great thermal barrier between the bottom of your feet and the ground or open air while on a treestand. By throwing a couple of heat packs down each leg, you can stay toasty warm.

The best warm weather boots you can afford, are great, but if you don't keep your feet dry, the power of the boot to keep you warm can be greatly reduced!

Although I don't do this enough, adding a piece of outdoor carpet to the top of your treestand platform can be a great way to keep the wind and open air off the bottom of your feet! Better yet, carrying a rolled up piece of carpet to place on the top of the stand when you hunt, can keep any ice or snow build up from creating the potential for extra crunchy sounds.

Can you find a pair of the old Micky Mouse style military issue boots from decades past? If so, they may be a very cheap, but high value, proven alternative to buying some of today's newest choices.

For over 30 years I've hunted with a hand warmer tube. I appreciate it's ability to carry my phone, grunt tube and gloves, however, it becomes a much more critical piece of my gear when the temperatures dip below freezing.

2. Warm Hands All Season Long

Hand warmer, hand warmer, hand warmer. Folks, I can't say enough about how a hand warmer changed my hunting all the way back to the mid 80s. I saw a fancy hand warmer muff at the old Dunham's Sporting Goods in Waterford, MI in the mid 80s, and although I couldn't afford it, I just had to have one. The somewhat easy solution? I had my mom sew a multi-layer wool replica for me, with a giant safety pin attached. That homemade hand warmer probably saved my teenage fingers over 30 years ago, and I can say the same for my much older set of digits, to this day. I would estimate that I have worn a hand warmer muff 95% of the time during every hunt since, and I can strongly recommend that you follow the same practice for never getting cold fingers.

Keeping your hands warm is as easy as wearing a high quality muff every time that you head to the woods. I even wear mine during the early season as a way to carry my cell phone, grunt tube, extra camera batteries, diabetes gel packs, SD cards and gloves. By layering a Gore-Tex leg gator around the muff when it is cold and rainy, and by adding up to 2 large heat packs when needed, you will find you only need to wear thin gloves to stay warm in literally, any temperature.

By always having a free hand when walking in or out, one hand is always in my muff and toasty warm. By rotating hands, I can keep them warm even on frigid, highly exposed walks in or out of the stand.

Wearing extra heavy mittens on the way in or out of your stand can be the perfect choice for sub-zero temps. However, don't do what I have done! Back in the late 90s, I placed my sweated up heavy gloves on my lower tree steps to stay until I climbed back down. Of course, they froze and I had nothing warm to place my hands in for the walk out of the woods, with temps in single digits. That 30-minute walk was likely one of my top 5 coldest times for my fingers, any time in my life. After that fairly dumb mistake, I now have a much better practice of placing the warm gloves against my chest, under my outer layer. That keeps my "walk-in" gloves or mittens toasty warm and also adds another layer against my core.

3. Critical Core Warming Tips

When it comes to extremely cold weather, pants just don't cut it. If you want to stay warm in the worst of conditions, bibs aren't just an option - they are a necessity! Bibs allow you to manage the temperature of your core, which is the lifeblood of your entire body.

Using bib overalls keeps the cold air sealed out of your core. Attempting to tuck tails of shirts, and cover the top of your pants with coats and other layers, only allows air to seal in around the lifeblood of your body's entire heat system.

By layering vests and other mid-weight core management pieces, you can add an outstanding compliment to wearing bib overalls.

Adding heat packs against your chest and belly when needed, creates the opportunity for cutting the chill during long stretches on a treestand or in a blind. I like adding the heat packs if, and when needed, so I can enjoy the heat and literally feel the chill being chased away.

Quality long johns and base layers of fleece or other high tech fabrics from a hunting industry leading company like Sitka Gear, is a critical first step in insuring that your entire core, as well as the rest of your body, can stay warm. Quality base layers also have the ability to wick moisture away from your skin throughout your entire sit, which is even more important than an extra layer of insulation.

4. All Weather Head Warming System

Like the hands, there is no excuse for not keeping your head warm every time you enter the deer woods. It doesn't take a huge amount of money, it is critically important, and by using various types of head warming layers, you can expect to stay warm anywhere, during any condition.

Like my hand warmer muff, I always have a face mask in the woods with me. Whether I am trying to take the shine off my face or stay warm, using various thicknesses of face masks are the first easy step in the entire process.

The core Heavy Weight Hoody by Sitka Gear is something that I wear nearly every time I enter the woods! With a built-in face mask and hood, it is an essential piece of clothing that can be used at every temperature. By adding a 2nd layer of face mask underneath, you are well on your way to staying warm in near-freezing temperatures.

Once you have used an adequate amount of face mask coverage, the next step is to add either a high tech stocking cap, or for the harshest of conditions, a Gore-Tex insulated cap combo.

Make sure if you are bowhunting, to always practice with the amount of layers you will be hunting with, against your face. For right-handed shooters, a thick mask will push your anchor point to the right, causing you to shoot left at 20 yards by up to several inches. Using a kisser button only magnifies the issue, which is why I do not recommend a kisser button when hunting deer.

Don't laugh! Even if it means matching decades old mickey mouse style boots with the latest and greatest gear technology, I suggest that you do whatever it takes to stay warm in the treestand.

Conclusion

Warm hunting clothes are something that you should never skimp on. In fact, high quality clothes should not only last you personally for decades, but should last long enough to be passed down to younger generations of hunters to keep them safe, warm and dry while hunting. My own kids just don't realize what I went through to stay warm over 30 years ago, and I often wonder if they would have had the passion to keep hunting, if they experienced the level of frozen toes, hands, head and core that I personally had to endure. Today's new lines of clothing options are incredible for not only helping you stay warm in the harshest of deer hunting conditions, but to be able to actually draw and shoot your bow with ease! Don't miss out on the best days of the season because they are bitter and brutal. Instead, you can hunt extreme cold weather whitetail opportunities in both comfort and functionality. Great gear is worth the expense and can help you bowhunt at higher levels than you could have ever imagined a couple of decades ago.

Chapter 15

Forecasting Your Next Sit of a Lifetime

It is now time to grab your own level of All Weather Whitetail success. There is no need for you to rely on the whims of neighbors, wildlife regulations or predators to define your hunt. Instead, by planning your hunts around the weather, you can take control of the consistency of your hunting opportunities. Better yet, when you control your hunt, you also have a great opportunity to control the quality of the herd that you hunt. The weather forecast is a powerful tool based on a set of physical ingredients that carry the power to create chaos in our world, let alone a day in the life of a monster buck. There are several ways that you can insulate the potential of your herd and hunting efforts from the outside influences of neighbors, wildlife regulations and predators, by using the weather forecast to guide you to success.

Neighborly Concerns

Let's face it; hunters often hunt in less than ideal circumstances. I have experienced for decades, that every time that you step foot in the whitetail woods, you reduce your chances for hunting success. The reason that deer gravitate to parks, golf courses and neighborhood set-aside land, is the same reason that they leave your favorite hunting grounds – Pressure! Whitetails have an uncanny way of finding a corner of the neighborhood that has little to no hunting pressure. When you learn to follow the best days to hunt based on the weather, you set yourself, your land and the local herd up for experiencing the best that high level hunting and herd management has to offer. So many lands are burned-out well before the high value days even have a chance to express themselves. By being patient and carefully choosing exactly when to head to your favorite treestand based on high value weather predictions, your chance of success is often magnified by neighbors who have chosen to prematurely hunt during low probability days. When you are the only one exercising patience in the neighborhood, your ability to attract, hold, protect, grow and hunt a herd that is seeking shelter from people pressure, is outstanding!

Wildlife Regulations

I hear about the same pattern over and over again: too many deer permits, too few deer and too many buck permits. It is too convenient at times, to blame wildlife officials and changing regulations, for the decrease in deer numbers. However, this is a very unfair approach because it ignores the power that hunters have to regulate and take control of the lowest hole in the bucket - Hunting pressure! Whether you are attempting to ward off the effects of neighboring hunting pressure or decreasing deer numbers, plugging the lowest hole in the bucket of quality herds and hunting opportunity, has to take place first. By reducing hunting pressure by cheating your efforts towards only the best days to be in the woods, don't be surprised that regardless of changes in the hunting regulations, you can increase or decrease the number of deer that reside during the season on your land simply by limiting your intrusions. Less is more when it comes to creating a quality herd and hunt, and the weather can guide you to whitetail success on many different levels.

Predators

Over hunting your favorite whitetail woods, combined with a high population of predators, can reduce your overall deer numbers to zero pretty quickly! Having a strong population of predators on the lands that you hunt, is not that different from sharing your hunting grounds with another hunter or two. Unless you practice aggressive predation control, the presence of predators remains a constant source of negative pressure on your land. Without shooting every single predator that moves, learning how to pressure your land only at times that offer you the highest levels of hunting potential, is the best way to guard against predators. I know it sounds like a broken record, but the patience needed to choose and hunt the best days to be in the woods, is an outstanding method to reduce your hunting pressure, and it can even help you ward off the effects of predation.

Using the weather forecast can help you not only take a higher level of control of your hunt but it has the power to help you balance your time afield with your time at home and in your career.

Conclusion

Hunting pressure is the most destructive factor during the hunting season. Of course, All Weather Whitetail Hunting doesn't eliminate hunting pressure, noisy neighbors, aggressive wildlife regulations or predators, but the weather forecast creates a system of hunting management that allows you to take a much higher level of control for your whitetail success. I've found throughout the decades that the weather forecast allows me to consistently shoot more bucks by sitting on the couch, while the local deer herd seeks refuge within the hunting grounds that I enjoy. Whether you are hunting a 40-acre chunk of private land pressured by neighbors, or a remote public land hotspot subject to excessive numbers of hunters and predators, the weather forecast can create much more than just a great day to sit in your favorite treestand.

Conclusion

After reading this book, the conclusion of my 2016 Ohio public land hunt should come as no surprise! The mature target buck that we had the most trail cam footage of, came barreling down the ridge and only 20 yards to my left, as he aggressively chased the doe and fawn through the greenbriar. While the end of the primary rut was almost over, the high value Post Rut precision sit prospects, were not. I Believe that was my 25th public land buck kill. Although each and every one of those hunts are burned into a collection of memories to last a lifetime, the entire hunt from the drive, to the recovery, to the weather, was one of my most rewarding hunts ever – on public or private land!

A 40-degree temperature drop and a 30mph wind was such a major deerfront opportunity that after Dante's buck, I followed the storm for nearly a 700-mile trek and a ½ hour of sleep in the truck, to make sure that I could capture the same high value weather sit forecast, 2 days in a row. I did so because the odds were severely on my side. The weather can create odds that are that predictable, and I have been experiencing the results of playing those odds nearly every season, for decades.

I want you to experience those same results too! One of the reasons for the extreme level of passion to continue my writings is that I am truly excited to assist others in finding the same level of success based on the same collection of hunting, herd and habitat strategies, that I have enjoyed for so many years. I am sure that you can relate but, even though this nimrod hasn't always closed the deal, nearly every target buck that I have pursued since the early 90s, has been delivered to me by following the roller coaster of hunting season deerfronts. My true hope is that you can recognize that using the weather to forecast your next hunt of a lifetime is as much of a way of hunting life than it is a hunting strategy. I'm not sure that I would have the career that I do, if it wasn't for the option to use the weather forecast, to efficiently balance my whitetail adventures along with the amount of time that it takes to an establish a successful small business.

Even if you are a full-time whitetail professional who can hunt whenever you desire, you can still use the weather as a road map to capture high value hunting experiences, all season long. However, if you are like 99% of the rest of the hunting population that has to manage the resources of time and money wisely, the strategies offered to you in this book, can assist you in much more than simply hanging a monster buck on the living room wall. In conclusion, the forecast features a high-powered collection of deerfront strategies that I encourage you to practice, hone and master, so that you too can seize the decades of enjoyment that a whitetail weather life has to offer.

Ohio public land buck November 20, 2016. 40 degree temperature drop, 30 mile per hour wind decrease and clearing skies.